D0227762

Effective
Presentation

■

The Institute of Management (IM) is at the forefront of management development and best management practice. The Institute embraces all levels of management from students to chief executives. It provides a unique portfolio of services for all managers, enabling them to develop skills and achieve management excellence.

If you would like to hear more about the benefits of membership, please write to Department P, Institute of Management, Cottingham Road, Corby NN17 ITT.

This series is commissioned by the Institute of Management Foundation.

Effective presentation

■ ■ ■

ANTONY JAY
& ROS JAY

the Institute
of Management

FOUNDATION

PITMAN
PUBLISHING

Learning Resources
Centre

PITMAN PUBLISHING
128 Long Acre, London WC2E 9AN

A Division of Pearson Professional Limited

First published in Great Britain 1996

British Library Cataloguing in Publication Data
A CIP catalogue record for this book can be obtained
from the British Library.

ISBN 0 273 62194 7

10 9 8 7 6 5 4 3

Typeset by Pantek Arts, Maidstone
Printed and bound in Great Britain by
Bell and Bain Ltd, Glasgow

*The Publishers' policy is to use paper manufactured
from sustainable forests.*

The Authors

ANTONY JAY, formerly Chairman of Video Arts (the world's largest video training company) and author of *Yes Minister*, is a recognised and respected authority on presentations.

ROS JAY is a business editor and well known writer whose books include: *Build a Great Team!*, *Low Cost Marketing* and *How to Write Proposals and Reports That Get Results*.

v

Contents

■ ■ ■

ix

Preface

■ ■ ■

It was in about 1964 that I discovered presentations. Until then I had been a full-time television producer and writer at the BBC, believing that I was one of a very small group of people who were grappling with the problem of employing a wide range of audio-visual techniques to present facts, ideas and arguments. But in 1964 I became a freelance and quite soon I was invited to produce a presentation for an industrial company.

From then on the pace quickened, and I began to realise that all over the world thousands, maybe tens of thousands, of presentations were being given and attended every day. Research groups presenting new projects to development committees, salespeople presenting products to customers, advertising agencies presenting campaign ideas to clients, boards presenting new organisations or policies to executives, and all of them presenting things to the press and the public.

Almost as soon as the extent of this new industry dawned on me, I realised that it was rooted in exactly the same craft that I had been practising for the past ten years. Of course, there were no television cameras or telecine machines or microphone booms, but these are only the trappings and suits of television anyway. At the heart of my kind of factual, documentary television was the essential problem of the presentation: how to put over to small groups of people (the television audience is made up of small groups, too, even if there are several million of them) new facts and ideas, in an attractive, interesting and persuasive way, by the simultaneous use of words and pictures.

Obviously I started with something of an advantage: this problem had been my full-time professional occupation for ten years, and I had discussed almost every aspect of it endlessly with my colleagues on production teams. Moreover, for six of those years I had worked on a forty-minute, five-nights-a-week news/documentary/current affairs programme calling, at one time or another, on every audio-visual technique and narrative device.

Even so it came as a surprise, when going outside the walls of the television studio, to discover how little thought or discussion had been given to the problems and principles of presentations by those who had to devise and make them. Industry, which seemed to be flooded with expert advisers on cost accounting, work study, operational research, media selection, press relations, resource management, production control, personnel motivation and almost every other specialist and even non-specialist activity, had desperately few helpers of even the most modest competence in the field of presentations, and no corpus of professional knowledge at all.

For this reason it is hardly surprising that it was difficult to go to any presentation in the 1960s without encountering the most elementary errors of conception and execution. Much more surprising was the patient tolerance of the audiences who sat through them in charitable silence with a politeness that approached the heroic.

It is now over twenty-five years since I started producing and advising on presentations, and for most of that time I have found that there are certain basic points which I have had to make again and again – points which we hammered out in the 1950s in session after session of programme autopsies until we had forged, at least to our own satisfaction, a basic grammar of audio-visual communication.

If anyone has picked up this book in the hope of a crackling philosophical discourse on the nature of human communication in modern industrial society, I advise them to put it down at once. It is no more than a brief and very humble operating manual for those who, at some time or another, have to present ideas, decisions, facts or proposals to others in a context which demands something slightly more prepared and worked out than a chat over a drink, and who believe that it is worth spending some time and trouble to achieve maximum clarity, conciseness, impact and persuasion: or at least to avoid alienation, catastrophe and humiliation.

The technological apparatus available to today's presenter has increased dramatically since the first edition of this book was published, but experience suggests that the basic understanding of communication techniques and presentation skills has hardly advanced at all. This means that the revision has not involved any omissions or excisions of points that have become too well known or obvious since the first publication in 1971.

In recent years I have had less to do with the world of management and marketing. Happily this has coincided with my daughter Ros entering the business and establishing herself as a management writer. She has brought to the original book her own much more recent experience of the world of presentations, and has also pointed out (and repaired) a number of significant omissions from it. She has also edited and reorganised much of the earlier material, and we have both added a number of further hints and tips which we have picked up over the years. The result is a much clearer and more comprehensive guide than the first edition; whether it will last for another 20-odd years is something we will have to wait and see.

Antony Jay

Somerset, November 1995

Acknowledgements

■ ■ ■

Since the first publication of this book in 1971 I have written two booklets on presentation skills for Video Arts Ltd: *Slide Rules* and *Making Your Case*. They were written to accompany the presentation training films *'Can We Please Have That The Right Way Round?'* and *Making Your Case*, and I would like to take this opportunity to thank the company for permission to include the material from those booklets in this revised and updated edition.

I would also like to thank Sally Deung for letting me draw on her expertise in dress and personal presentation, which forms a substantial part of Chapter 8.

XV

Introduction

■ ■ ■

What is a presentation?

■ ■ ■

To start with, it is not a lesson, and presenters cannot think of their role in terms of a teacher's. None of the audience is going to sit an examination and answer questions on what they have been told. The presenter cannot set them homework, or give individual attention to the slower pupils, or stop and give a quick test to see who has been paying attention. Moreover, one of the most important of the teacher's techniques is almost always denied to the presenter – the technique of involving the class, making them do things for themselves, keeping them busy. There is, of course, a strong element of presentation in class instruction, for which I hope the following chapters will be useful, but handling the class is more important and deserves a book which I am certainly not competent to write.

Less obvious, and for that reason perhaps more important, is the fact that a presentation is not a lecture. They look alike, there is rarely any class activity in a lecture, and lecturers employ all the visual techniques discussed in this book. Nevertheless there is a crucial difference and it lies in the reason why the audience is there.

Why is the audience there?

■ ■ ■

A lecturer can reasonably assume (even if the best of them do not) that the audience arrives with a desire, or at least a need, to know what the lecturer is going to tell them. A presenter's audience is, in almost every case, invited by them or their organisation; the presenter's need to impart information is usually greater than the audience's need to receive it. Moreover, lecturers are usually to some extent the servants of a syllabus. If something is particularly complicated they just have to take extra time to try and elucidate it: they do not have the same freedom as the presenter to choose what to put in and what to leave out.

If one must find a parallel from another profession, a presenter is much closer to an advocate than to a teacher or lecturer. A presentation is an exercise in persuasion. Of course there are other ingredients – the communication of information and ideas – but a presentation takes place in order to persuade a person or group of persons to:

■ adopt or revise an attitude;
■ accept or modify an opinion;
■ take or refrain from taking an action or decision.

Of course teachers and lecturers have the same need to persuade, but in a presentation it is more overt.

The relationship with the audience
■ ■ ■

In most presentations, too, the normal speaker–audience relationship is reversed. If someone stands up on their own to address a crowd of others, there is an implication that their status is in some way superior – this is dealt with more fully in Chapter 7 – but in a presentation it is usually the other way round; the speaker addresses the audience respectfully as a subordinate among people of higher status. He or she cannot demand their attention – the most they can do is to deserve it. A normal consequence of this is that the duration of the presentation is restricted. A lecturer may ask 'How long does the subject need?', but the presenter's first question is usually 'How long can the audience spare?'

The logic of limited time leads to certain inescapable conclusions. Obviously the presenter, like the lecturer, wants to use the time to maximum advantage, and this involves taking trouble. The lecturer can share the trouble with his or her class, give them extra reading, writing or practical work, or force them to concentrate hard during the lecture; the presenter takes all the trouble to save the audience trouble, and makes things hard for him or herself so that they may be easy for them.

Sound and vision
■ ■ ■

One consequence of this is the need for visual aids. You cannot compress words beyond a certain limit without losing the comprehension and interest of your audience, but a judicious use of pictures can communicate the same information better.

> **PICTURES CAN BE BETTER THAN WORDS**
>
> ■ Faster
> ■ More effective
> ■ Easier to remember

And once visual aids are included, the exposition starts to become more formal in the strict sense of having to keep to a prearranged form. A talk can wander about in a general way on the basis of a few points in the speaker's head or a few notes on a crib-card, but presenters depart from the order of a slide sequence at their peril.

It may seem that the presentation is a form of communication which is walled about with restrictions and loaded with burdens. It does, however, have one liberating factor: it is usually only required to be a prelude to further discussion and exposition. If it fails, that further discussion will not take place, but if it succeeds, the audience to whom it was given will want to study the subject in more detail. Its objective is limited; it does not have to be comprehensive. Usually a presentation is successful if it arouses curiosity and stimulates a desire for more information: the desire can be satisfied in other ways and at other times.

1
■ ■ ■

Planning the presentation: thinking it out

1

Before starting to write a presentation you need to be clear about its purpose. Once you have set a precise objective, and worked out exactly who your audience is, what they know already and what they want to learn, you can start to plan the presentation.

The planning stage involves working out who is going to say what, for how long, and in what order. This process is vital, and worth putting thought and effort into. It will give the presentation a strong skeleton structure which will render all the later fleshing out far easier and quicker.

It is a general law applicable to any project that the earlier a mistake is made the more profoundly it affects the whole project and the harder it is to recover from. Presentations are no exception. If there is a misconception, or an omission, or an error of intent built into the beginning of a presentation, then all the subsequent time, thought and work are doomed.

For this reason there should be a fair amount of exploratory discussion, with at least three people, at the very beginning. In Chapter 3 we deal with the subject of what meetings are necessary and who should attend; at the moment we are concerned with what must be done.

Although this section deals with the presentation as a whole, the individual presenters each have to follow the separate stages when they approach their subsection of the whole presentation.

2

Start from first principles
■ ■ ■

Formulate a precise objective

The first question to ask is why you are giving the presentation at all. It is easy to come up with a vague, general answer; the aim is to narrow it down to a single sentence defining a precise and limited objective.

You can say, 'To improve the company's return on employed assets', but that is everyone's business all the time. You can say, 'To sell more computer software', which is getting warmer, but what is the whole sales team for? All right, 'To remove doubts and misgivings about menu-driven computer software from the minds of potential customers'. Which doubts and misgivings? That it doesn't work? That it is too expensive? That people won't use it?

Try to make your objective as clear as possible

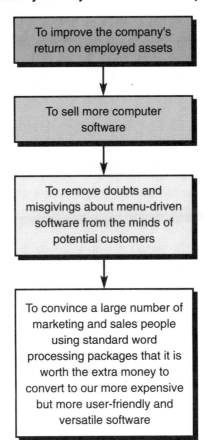

3

The more of this sort of questioning you subject yourself to at this stage, the more you sharpen the point of the whole presentation. It is worth writing out your final objective in a single sentence, 'To convince a large number of marketing and sales people using standard word processing packages that it is worth the extra money to convert to our more expensive but more user-friendly and versatile software', and making sure that everyone sees it, and sees it the moment they are recruited to the presentation team.

This objective should become the touchstone against which you test anything that may or may not deserve inclusion in your presentation.

Identify the audience

The second part of thinking it out, although separate, is intimately bound up with the first, and you cannot begin to formulate any part of the presentation until this too has been resolved. I have to put them on paper consecutively, but in your mind they have to proceed in parallel.

If the last section asked, 'What are we trying to convey?', this section asks, 'To whom are we trying to convey it?' For this you have to try and get inside the mind of your audience.

All this has to be thrashed out just as thoroughly as the objective. If you are in serious doubt, it is worth having a session with someone who will be one of the audience, or at least comes from the same group (e.g. sales manager, publicity officer, marketing executive), to try to find out from them the level of interest, information, understanding, experience, prejudice and resistance that you should expect to find in your audience.

4

INSIDE THE AUDIENCE'S MIND

- What are they thinking about the subject?
- How much do they already know about computers?
- What is the level of their technical interest and understanding?
- How much have they used computers in the past?
- How up to date are they with the latest software?
- Is it the concept of upgrading their software that they are resisting, or are they simply deciding between us and our competitors?

Finally, you should be able to formulate another key sentence – the one which expresses the final impression you want to leave in the mind of your audience when the presentation ends. Again, you must limit it: should it be, 'I must remember to order one of the things tomorrow morning' or just, 'Perhaps these things can help us after all – I must set up a committee to look at it properly'?

These two thought processes may sound obvious, and indeed everybody who plans a presentation goes through them in some sort of way. The reason for emphasising them here is that in most cases the process is carried out in a hasty and desultory manner, and abandoned while the objective is still inadequately formulated and the audience too vaguely identified.

For a successful presentation, at least two hours need to be set aside for questions, suggestions, arguments and the formulation of exact objectives – two exhausting hours of hard thinking. Considering how much more time is going to be spent on scripts, rehearsals and visual aids in the days to come, this is a small amount to allot to constructing the foundations on which everything else will be built.

The ingredients
∎ ∎ ∎

5

Quite simply, what shall we include? This is the obvious bit that everyone can do. Here are a few tips:

- Simply for the production discipline, write down the point each section is making. Not simply 'range', but 'range of programmes now available, and further programmes in preparation'.

- Even at this early stage, put duration against each section and subsection – it helps to give early warning of overcrowding.

- It can help to sort out the various possible ingredients into A, B and C columns: A for what must be included; B for what ought to be; and C for what it would be worth saying if there were time.

- Having noted all the points you want to include, form them into a logical sequence in which the points you are trying to make succeed each other most naturally.

If you like you can suggest speakers, if there is to be more than one, and durations in the margin. The following example will show what I mean.

Sample logical sequence

---

1 CHAIRMAN'S INTRODUCTION

(a) Computing now universal. Computers used by operators with no specialist computing knowledge – so future trend is for user-friendly programmes.

(b) Bottleneck in computing not hardware or software, but skill of operator. But non-computer staff want easy system so they can put concentration into main function (marketing or sales).

(c) Menu-driven programmes easier to learn, harder to make mistakes, so computer works for staff, not staff for computer.

Total 10 mins
Running total 10 mins

2 SALES DIRECTOR

(d) Will demonstrate in a moment. First, the economics. Cost of programme. Additional benefits – training, emergency hotline, optional extras.

(e) Conversational relationship with computer. Computer asks the questions.

Demonstration of basic programme

(f) Outline add-on and additional programmes available. Other software planned for near future.

Total 20 mins
Running total 30 mins

3 SENIOR PROGRAMMER

(g) Brief explanation of Desktop Publishing section of programme. What it does and how easy it is.

(h) Producing simple sales and publicity literature with Desktop Publishing.

Demonstration: Desktop publishing   *Total 15 mins*
Running total 45 mins

4 CUSTOMER (MARKETING DIRECTOR)

(i) Practical applications. Teething troubles. Lessons learnt. Pitfalls. Summary of advantages to date. Planned developments for future.

Total 10 mins
Running total 55 mins

---

5 CHAIRMAN'S SUMMARY

(j) Growth of user-friendly computing. Makes it possible to use computers to do far more.

(k) Better staff retention because more motivated. Comparative cost/ benefit analysis with using outside agencies for Desktop Publishing. Flexibility – scope to add on and upgrade at minimal cost. End story.

Total 10 mins
Running total 1 hr 5 mins

Once the logical sequence is worked out, everyone should have a copy of it. It is important that all those who are going to give parts of the presentation should be well acquainted with everybody else's theme as well before they start to think about what they want to say – it is a great help in preventing gaps or overlap.

7

Structure
■ ■ ■

If the first two stages have been properly completed, we know what we want to say, why, in what order, and to whom. Now we have to decide how to structure it.

Surely we have done that already with our logical sequence? No, we have not. The chief purpose of that was to clear up in our own minds the progression of the argument. We will probably follow the thread of it, more or less, but we now have to add something else: the storyteller's art. So far all we have produced is a logical argument: we now have to turn it into an interesting talk or series of talks.

The word 'talk' is significant, and talk is the subject of Chapter 4. This is a spoken presentation and not a written paper. For this reason, any presenters who are inexperienced in writing for speech should, when they have structured their talks, speak them into a tape-recorder and have them transcribed, rather than write them out.

The preface

Almost every presentation requires some sort of preface. Exactly what elements it should contain will obviously depend on circumstances – you do not have to explain who you are if you are addressing your own department (or if you do have to, there is something wrong that no presentation will put right).

The preface has a double value – it establishes certain important facts, and it also helps to ease presenters into their relationship with the audience by means of 'neutral' material that everyone can accept and agree with. The longer you keep everyone nodding, the better, as long as they don't nod off.

There are five elements to a full preface (a single sentence may be enough for each).

8

- *Welcoming courtesies* – simply thanking people for giving up time and hoping they will feel it is well spent.

- *Self-identification* – your name and job, your background if relevant ('I worked in the aircraft industry myself for two years, though not of course at your exalted level ...') and any details about colleagues who are with you.

- *The intention* – what you are proposing to explain, suggest or demonstrate at this presentation. This has to be angled towards the benefits they can expect from what you are presenting – not 'Tell you about our new GZ180', but 'Show you how our GZ180 could provide you with a quicker and more economical ...'. Everything should be presented in terms of their interest, not yours: not 'What I am going to tell you', but 'What I thought you would like to know'.

- *The route map* – how long the presentation will last, whether it will be in sections, will it all be here or will we be moving to another part of the building, does it include a video, will there be a break for coffee?

- *The rules of the road* – in particular, do you want people to interrupt if they have a question, or wait until the end of the session, or hold all questions until the end? They cannot know unless you tell them.

The first few minutes of the presentation are extremely important in a way that has nothing to do with its content. There is a folklore belief that you should always start with a joke: like so many folklore beliefs it is not true, but there is truth somewhere at the root of it. The fact is that every speaker needs some sort of acceptance from the audience: if they are to accept what you say, they need some grounds for believing that you are in most ways the same sort of person as them.

A good joke that is not obtrusively dragged in, that is relevant and amusing and gets a big laugh, is an excellent way of giving them this sense of all belonging to the same tribe (see Chapter 7). However, a joke that fails has exactly the reverse effect and may be very hard to recover from. An opening joke is therefore particularly dangerous with very small audiences, with unfamiliar audiences, or if ever you have doubts about whether it will get the laugh you intend.

9

There are many alternatives to telling a joke, which will still help you to create an 'accepting' kind of atmosphere:

- any expression of genuine personal feelings;
- some honest self-revelation;
- a self-deprecating remark.

All of these approaches work because they show that you are just as ordinary as the rest of them, and not setting yourself up as a superior person. This, of course, applies not just for the start of the whole presentation, but also for each new presenter's opening remarks.

The core structure

Hold your breath and wait for a massive generalisation. Ready? Right: **all good presentations have the same structure.**

It is a simple, three-part structure, and the same as a symphony or a play: exposition, development, recapitulation; first movement, second movement, third movement; Act I, Act II, Act III; order demonstrated, order challenged, order re-established. You can embroider it in all sorts of ways, but if you abandon it – resorting, for example, to a string of unstructured and unconnected assertions – you will not hold your audience's attention for long.

For the purposes of a presentation, you can call the structure 'situation, complication, recommendation' and you will find that everything you have to say fits into one of those three sections. If there are several presenters, it is the overall presentation in its entirety which will fall into these three sections, though of course you may well find sometimes that one, or more, of the individual addresses is also clearer when it is structured in this way.

10

Situation

The members of an audience at the start of a presentation are like the horses before the start of the race – scattered all over the place and facing in different directions.

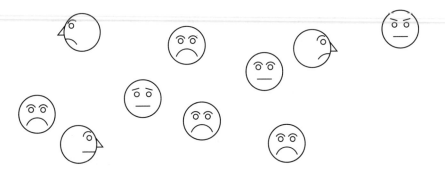

The starter at a race meeting has to bring them all up to the line together so that they start level and all go off in the right direction at the same time.

A presenter has to do much the same: if you gallop straight off you may hurtle along splendidly without realising that you left them all behind at the starting gate. So, you have to gather your audience together and connect yourself up to them.

Bringing an audience together

The way to do it is to outline the present situation: describe the way overseas distribution is currently organised, or the way the pattern of home demand has been changing, or the way we order stationery at the moment – whatever the purpose of your presentation, it is essential that everyone should start with the same knowledge, and important that you should demonstrate to them all that you know the situation and background. It also enables everyone to focus on the specific part of the present situation to which you are addressing yourself.

11

This does not only help comprehension: it also helps you to get accepted by the audience. By showing them that you understand their situation you are getting their confidence that you are in touch with them and worthy to be granted a further hearing.

This part of the presentation, establishing common ground, may take only a couple of sentences or it may need quite a long analysis of how things came to be the way they are, but some statement of the present situation has to be made and agreed upon. By all means ask them questions about the present situation and past history if you want to (this is more likely to be appropriate at smaller presentations): it helps you to angle the rest of your presentation more precisely to their needs, and a bit of two-way communication in the early stages can also be a valuable icebreaker.

Complication

This is where you introduce the need for change by showing why the present situation cannot continue, or why it would be unwise to continue it. There must be some significant change or danger or worry or opportunity, or you would not be making the presentation.

THERE MUST BE SOME REASON WHY THINGS CANNOT GO ON AS THEY ARE:

- Demand is shifting
- Staff are leaving
- Competitors are gaining
- Profits are falling
- Technology is changing
- Delays are lengthening
- Costs are rising
- Buildings are leaking

This is the stage at which you dig the hole in which you intend to plant your idea.

12 A computer salesman once explained to me, rather convincingly, why his job was very like a missionary's or an evangelist minister's. Both he and they, he said, succeeded by discovering or implanting some unease, guilt or fear in the person they were trying to convert. He himself did not deal in hell fire and torment, only in business rivals doing things cheaper, better or quicker and some people being left behind, but he felt that the principle was the same: nobody was interested in salvation until they had a fear of damnation.

I am not suggesting anything so extreme; nevertheless if your audience is rather cool it is a great help if you can make them aware, from the very start, of the ways in which what you are about to present is important to them. They arrive prepared to listen: by the end of the first ten minutes they should be wanting to know.

Recommendation

The two previous sections may be brief: this one forms the bulk of the presentation, and it is also the one you are least likely to omit. It may include evaluating alternatives, demonstrating products, describing services, meeting objections, comparing prices, adducing evidence, quoting examples, and is in fact what most people mean when they talk about 'a presentation'. But its success may well depend on how well you have prepared the ground in those first two sections which it is all too easy to omit.

Very often you will find that 'evaluating alternatives' is important enough to deserve a section on its own. You may also decide that your recommendation should itself be a choice of alternatives rather than a single take-it-or-leave-it proposal. Because of the importance of discussing alternatives, you may find it helpful to think in terms of a four-part structure, and if you add in your introduction and conclusion you can create a 6P alliterative mnemonic:

- Preface
- Position
- Problem
- Possibilities
- Proposal
- Postscript

13

Summary

The ending of a presentation, like the opening, is too important to be left to the mercy of chance or the whim of the moment. True, you may think of an improvement on your planned ending while you are speaking, but it is still vital to have a planned ending to improve on. This does not mean that it has to be long or complicated, only that it has to be worked out in advance and well rehearsed.

It is when working out your ending that you must go back to the original statement or intention. It is the objective of the presentation that dictates the ending. The ending will normally include:

- *a summary of the salient facts and arguments* and a reprise of the key visuals;
- *a recommendation* of a course of action;
- *a proposal for the next step*, if the recommendation is accepted, with target dates;

- *a description of the supporting literature* (if any) which you are now distributing;
- *thanks* for patient attention;
- *invitation to ask questions.*

Duration

Most people are worried that they will not have enough to say. There seems to be some sort of guilt about giving short measure. Consequently, the great danger at this stage is having too much. It is not a bad idea to use the A,B and C principle, and to mark each paragraph of your draft script (and other speakers' if any) with the appropriate grade. You can then cut the 'C' paragraphs without too much trouble. Cutting at the draft outline stage is easy, but it becomes more and more painful as time goes on, and further thought, time and care are put into it.

Always aim to run significantly short at this stage: more ideas will come in later, the presentations will 'spread' when the presenters actually use the visual aids, and so what if a morning's presentation is twenty minutes short? You've presumably said what you want, and the extra length of coffee and pre-lunch breaks won't upset anybody.

By contrast, a presentation that runs too long upsets everyone. People try to go too fast, anticipated breaks are delayed and curtailed, and it is always the more interesting but less essential parts that get cut, consequently making the whole presentation more indigestible.

Keep relating to the audience

The principle of connecting up with the audience also applies at the end of each section of every presentation. When a point is made and you reach a pause, think of the audience's mind again. What question or reflection will be in it now?

At this stage of course you only need a sentence or so ('This is all very well, but it doesn't answer the question ...'), but it is a

14

**PLANNING THE PRESENTATION:
THINKING IT OUT**

Before you start to write a presentation you need to get its purpose clear in your mind. Once you have set a precise objective, and worked out exactly who your audience is, what they know already and what they want to learn, you can start to plan the presentation.

This stage involves working out who is going to say what, for how long, and in what order. This planning process is vital, and worth putting thought and effort into. It will give the presentation a strong skeleton structure which will render all the later fleshing out far easier and quicker.

A

It is a general law applicable to any project that the earlier a mistake is made the more profoundly it affects the whole project and the harder it is to recover from. Presentations are no exception. If there is a misconception, or an omission, or an error of intent built into the beginning of a presentation, then all the subsequent time and thought and work are doomed.

B

For this reason there should be a fair amount of exploratory discussion, with at least three people, at the very beginning. Chapter 4 on The Schedule deals with the subject of what meetings are necessary and who should attend; at the moment we are concerned with what must be done.

Although this section deals with the presentation as a whole, the individual presenters each have to follow the separate stages when they approach their subsection of the whole presentation.

C 15

Start from first principles

Formulate precise objective
The first question to ask is why you are giving the presentation at all. It is easy to come up with a vague general answer; the aim is to narrow it down to a single sentence you can say "To improve the company's return on employed assets", but that is everyone's business all the time. You can say "To sell more computer software", which is getting warmer, but what is the whole sales team for? All right, "To remove doubts and misgivings about menu-driven computer software from the minds of potential customers". Which doubts and misgivings? That it doesn't work? That it is too expensive? That people won't use it?

The more of this sort of questioning you subject yourself to at this stage, the more you sharpen the point of the whole presentation. It is worth writing out your final objective in a single sentence "To convince a large number of marketing and sales people using standard word processing packages that it is worth the extra money to convert to our more expensive but more user-friendly and versatile software" and making sure that everyone sees it, and sees it the moment they are recruited to the presentation team.

A

This objective should become the touchstone against which you test anything that may or may not deserve inclusion.

B

A Must be included
B Ought to be included if possible
C Worth saying if there is time

very important structural sentence: it also serves another useful purpose, that of 'signposting', which is dealt with in Chapter 4, and it helps to prevent the presentation becoming an unbroken string of factual assertions, which after a time becomes very hard to listen to.

The value of narrative

If you see yourself in danger of falling into the factual assertion trap, remember the value of narrative. You may be describing a piece of equipment and find yourself saying, 'This part does this ... This part does this ...', and so on, in a number of different ways, for far too long.

You can often improve the structure enormously by turning it into a story: 'Designing the projector was an intriguing problem. To start with it had to be portable, so ... but that meant we couldn't ... so we tried ... finally we hit on ... then we ran into another snag ... meanwhile the optical group had come up with an ingenious ... ', and a dull specification can be turned into an interesting narrative.

Don't be too comprehensive

Remember that this is only a presentation. It does not have to be comprehensive. Build it only out of things that will interest the audience as a whole. Do not include anything tedious, or beyond most of them, or too detailed, because it 'ought' to be included, or because one or two may want to know. You can supply any amount of supporting documentation as handouts for them to study at their leisure, and refer them to it at the appropriate point.

Further practical decisions

At this stage you should also decide, if necessary:

- whom to invite;
- what size the audience should be (see Chapter 7);
- where to hold the presentation (see Chapter 8).

If these decisions are being made for you, say by a client who has asked you to make a presentation, you should try to discover the answers to these questions at this stage.

At this point you should not be worrying too much about visual aids. Of course it may be that some demonstration is integral to the presentation and will be built in from the start; but excellent presentations can be given with no visual aids whatever, whereas no amount of them can turn a badly conceived and badly structured presentation into a good one.

By now you should already have the makings of a good presentation; the purpose of visual aids is to make it even better. That is what the next chapter is about.

Action checklist

17

1 Set your precise objective in one sentence.
2 Identify your audience.
3 Establish what is the final impression you want to leave the audience with.
4 Decide what sections to include and what point each section is making.
5 Put sections into a logical order, with timings and speakers indicated.
6 Mark sections A, B and C in order of importance, to speed up cutting if it is necessary later.
7 Think of an opening that will get the audience on your side.
8 Use techniques such as questions and narrative to motivate the audience and make them want to listen.
9 If it applies, decide the size of your audience, and who to invite.
10 Decide where to hold the presentation.

Thought-starters

1 *Have you ever attended a presentation where you felt you couldn't relate to the speaker? Could you tell why?*

2 *What was the best presentation you have attended? Why was it so good?*

3 *How many openings to presentations you have heard do you remember? What made them memorable?*

4 *How far into listening to a presentation do you usually get before you have formed an opinion of the speaker?*

5 *How do you quantify the effectiveness of your presentations?*

.2

Planning the presentation: staging

This is the impresario stage. So far we have thought of the audience as listeners to an address. Now we start to see them as spectators at a show. We look for points where interest sags, where the argument is complicated or lengthy, and think how we can lift it to a higher attention and enjoyment level. We study the presentation to find the points where the most interesting items should be placed.

This stage has to be approached with care: it is demanding on time and thought and, if mishandled, it can turn what would have been a competent presentation into a disaster. But it can also upgrade a pedestrian presentation into a first-class one.

All right, so we have decided what to say and worked out an interesting way of saying it. Need we do any more planning work?

The answer is no. If we have done most things right so far, we have a good basic exposition and we could go ahead with it as it stands. But almost certainly we can do better. For example, by starting to think about visuals we can find ways of making what we say:

- more intelligible;
- more interesting;
- more vivid;
- more memorable.

20 We may even find ways of making it entertaining and enjoyable. Moreover, at the back of our minds there is a feeling which Dr Johnson once expressed: 'This was a good dinner enough, to be sure; but it was not a dinner to *ask* a man to.' We are afraid that although we have devised a good enough presentation, it is not a presentation to ask an audience to.

In fact, so long as we put the right sort of thought into what we say, and take the proper care over how we say it, those fears are often unfounded, and adding visuals just for visuals' sake will do more harm than good. Nevertheless, if we provide visible as well as audible evidence of the care and trouble we have taken, it is an additional act of courtesy to our audience; and it is more than likely that by adding another dimension to the presentation we can improve it significantly.

The difference here is purpose. If all changes and additions now made are made for worked-out reasons based on the audience's mood, they are likely to work. If made because 'we ought to make more of a presentation of it' they will destroy good work done so far. It is better to omit this stage than go through with it for the wrong reasons.

You still want to go on? Right. But don't say I didn't warn you.

On the whole, the longer the presentation the more important this stage becomes. Fifteen minutes, and you don't have to worry too much. Three hours, and this is a major part of the planning. Also, the larger the audience the more important is this part. Yet even shorter presentations to small audiences can be greatly improved by a proper impresario approach.

This approach should be directed towards seven key areas.

Texture

■ ■ ■

By this I only mean the different ways of addressing the audience. One presenter talking solidly, alone, and unaided, for two hours, represents an insufficiently varied texture. Texture is varied by overhead projector slides (OHPs), video, sound tapes, demonstrations, other visual aids, other speakers, questions, and indeed any other method of communication.

To study texture, forget about content and just look at what the audience is getting in terms of *means* of communication.

WHAT IS THE AUDIENCE GETTING?

- Is there too much solid talk at any point?
- Will they be punch drunk with slide sequences?
- Are the demonstrations wasted by being too close – could they be split up?
- Does it get too jumpy and bitty?

It's hard to write rules: what you need is an instinct for the boring. Once you've spotted a dull patch it's not too hard to do something. Drop it, for instance – and write it as a supporting document. Look for ingredients you have hitherto omitted because of low relevance-priority which you should now reinstate on interest-priority.

At this stage, be prepared to make cuts and order changes – but don't lose hold of the main purpose. You are studying the means of communication – but what is being communicated is still what matters. The medium is not the message. The medium is the envelope, and you are concerned with the letter inside.

A good practice is to go to a fairly big presentation that you're not particularly interested in, and mark each stage A, B or C, for interesting, adequate or dull. It's easier to be ruthlessly honest about other people's presentations. But you will start to develop an instinct which you can apply to your own efforts.

It ought to be said at this stage that really first-class speakers who know their subject and their audience can, in some circumstances, hold an audience spellbound for an hour or more. But all too few of us have or can call upon such talent, and all too many of us have to manage without.

22

Attention curve

■ ■ ■

This closely connects with texture. Psychologists have plotted how the attention of an audience or class varies during a forty-minute period. It starts high, drops fairly shallowly for the first ten minutes, then more steeply until it reaches its lowest point after about thirty minutes. Then it starts to rise steeply and is high again for the last five minutes.

There are four points which follow from this.

- A shorter 'period' – say 25 or 30 minutes – contains a higher percentage of high attention (Though of course too many short sections become self defeating.)

- Your most important points for the audience to remember must be at the beginning and end. In particular the last picture and sentence or phrase of each period, which stay in the mind for a little longer before new words and images are piled on top, are especially important. (You

Be prepared to make cuts

**PLANNING THE PRESENTATION:
THINKING IT OUT**

Before you start to write a presentation you need to get its purpose clear in your mind. Once you have set a precise objective, and worked out exactly who your audience is, what they know already and what they want to learn, you can start to plan the presentation.

This stage involves working out who is going to say what, for how long, and in what order. This planning process is vital, and worth putting thought and effort into. It will give the presentation a strong skeleton structure which will render all the later fleshing out far easier and quicker.

It is a general law applicable to any project that the earlier a mistake is made the more profoundly it affects the whole project and the harder it is to recover from. Presentations are no exception. If there is a misconception, or an omission, or an error of intent built into the beginning of a presentation, then all the subsequent time and thought and work are doomed.

For this reason there should be a fair amount of exploratory discussion, with at least three people, at the veryy beginning. Chapter 4 on The Schedule deals with the subject of what meetings are necessary and who should attend; at the moment we are concerned with what must be done. *CUT*

Although this section deals with the presentation as a whole, the individual presenters each have to follow the separate stages when they approach their subsection of the whole presentation. *CUT*

Start from first principles

Formulate precise objective
The first question to ask is why you are giving the presentation at all. It is easy to come up with a vague, general answer; the aim is to narrow it down to a single sentence.
You can say "To improve the company's return on employed assets", but that is everyone's business all the time.
You can say "To sell more computer software", which is getting warmer, but what is the whole sales team for? All right, "To remove doubts and misgivings about menu-driven computer software from the minds of potential customers". Which doubts and misgivings? That it doesn't work? That it is too expensive? That people won't use it?

The more of this sort of questioning you subject yourself to at this stage, the more you sharpen the point of the whole presentation. It is worth writing out your final objective in a single sentence "To convince a large number of marketing and sales people using standard word processing packages that it is worth the extra money to convert to our more expensive but more user-friendly and versatile software" and making sure that everyone sees it, and sees it the moment they are recruited to the presentation team.

This objective should become the touchstone against which you test anything that may or may not deserve indictaion *CUT*

23

---

can add further emphasis by the length of your pause after an important point.)

■ Since attention diminishes after the first ten minutes it is after that period, until it climbs again, that the greatest attention must be paid to texture variation and all other devices to revive and retain attention.

■ The audience's attention will not rise towards the end of a session unless they know they are coming to the end of it.

Typical attention curve

Duration of presentation

Giving the audience advance notice of the structure of the presentation is dealt with in Chapter 4.

Breaks and session lengths
■ ■ ■

Again, this is closely related to texture and attention. A question session is not a break – it is a texture variation and is dealt with in Chapter 7. A break is when the audience can get up out of their seats.

First of all, try and think how many times you have been sorry that a seminar or presentation has reached a break. Now, think how many times you have been glad. If you're honest, the ratio is probably 1:10,000.

So breaks are a high point, and most presentations have too few. However, sometimes they are too long. It is much better to have two of ten minutes than one of twenty. A morning presentation of three hours is much better divided by two short refreshment breaks, one after the first hour and another after the second, than by a single one (even if longer) after an hour and a half.

Finally, try and make each session end on a high note, if only to have the audience saying to each other 'Quite good, isn't it?' over their coffee.

If sessions are not of equal length, then in principle the longest should be first and the shortest last, to combat the cumulative effect of successive sessions.

A peep behind the curtain
■ ■ ■

This does not apply quite so much to the very large presentation with the full printed programme, but in all other cases you have to remember that although *you* know what is coming, the audience does not. So, always cheer them up by telling them if there are some goodies in store.

GIVE THE AUDIENCE SOMETHING TO LOOK FORWARD TO

■ In just a moment I'll be showing you some interesting pictures we took ...'

■ 'I've got one of the machines here, and later on I'll see if I can get this effect ...'

■ This has in fact been filmed, and during this session you'll be seeing ...'

25

The mere presence of interesting looking boxes on the table, or of easels with flip charts, perks up interest wonderfully.

Remember, too, that attention peaks as you move over to start a demonstration, so between the 'Right, let's see if we can start the machine up ...' and the actual turning of the switch is an excellent moment to make a point you want everyone to take in.

Audience participation
■ ■ ■

Apart from the fact that there are no disciplinary sanctions, it is the absence of 'class activity', of the audience's participation, that makes the great difference between a lesson and a presentation. Participation, trying it out for yourself, is at the root of instruction. Because it is not there, the presenter is perhaps closer to the professional entertainer than to the teacher. But, having said that, it does not mean that the presenter should not jump at any chance which arises to involve the audience.

A joke is the most obvious example. A joke is not funny until it is laughed at, it is completed by the laugh, and by laughing the audience is participating in the joke. The television studio audience is a part of the show in a way that the viewers sitting at home smiling quietly to themselves are not.

But a joke that is not laughed at is a major disaster, and not everyone has the confidence or the technique to go for laughs. So, what else is there? Well, sometimes you can get mental activity going on the lines of 'How many wheels can you see in this picture?', but it doesn't happen much. There is, however, one opportunity which is too often neglected, and that is to give them something to hold – and if possible to keep.

Any small, cheap object which is reasonably relevant will do – a sample of your revolutionary new waterproof material, a small but vital component from one of your machines, an example of what your latest printing technique can achieve – these can be helpful and interesting, and a most valuable variant. You don't have to deal them out to everyone – a pack to pass along each row is enough. It gets harder with over a hundred people, but you can make up a small folder and put one on each seat in advance.

Impact
■　■　■

It can be helpful to think of visual aids as falling into three categories:

- explanatory;
- corroborative;
- impact.

You will have included your explanatory visuals from the start. They are the ones you cannot really manage without –

the sort of thing that it is impossible to explain in words, but is easy with a picture or diagram or model.

When you were thinking about texture and the attention curve you started looking for corroborative visuals. They were not a structural necessity, but they gave useful visual evidence, they backed up your argument, and they helped to lift the interest at a point where it was likely to be flagging.

Impact visuals are the ones that are most often forgotten. They answer the question, 'What pictures do we want the audience to carry away in their minds?' Quite possibly they will be pictures already used for explanatory or corroborative reasons, but very probably they will not. These need to be thought out with great care and placed in key positions – often first or last thing in their session, and perhaps left on show through the subsequent break.

There is an old proverb 'I hear and forget, I see and remember, I do and understand'. A presentation audience has not much scope for doing and understanding, but it will do a great deal of hearing and forgetting. It will, however, remember what it sees. You must make sure it sees everything you want it to remember.

27

Under the heading of 'impact' comes all those devices for waking the audience up, surprising them, and making them more alert and receptive. The best *coup de théâtre* I know of is the army officer's lecture about surprise in warfare. He announced the subject, placed a tiny squib on the table and got out his matchbox. As he was opening it, an accomplice detonated the most enormous maroon at the *back* of the audience. They leapt into the air as one, and three points about surprise (deception about time, deception about place, deception about strength) were indelibly engraved on their memories.

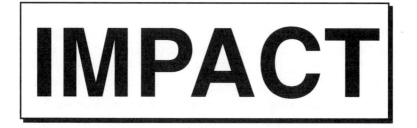

Casting

■ ■ ■

Who should deliver the presentation? To start with, should it be one person or several? On the whole I am for variety, so long as there is some logic in it. If the audience cannot see why B should have taken over from A at this stage, then it would have been better for A to have done it all; but so long as it is clear that we are now in an area where B has more skill or knowledge, or experience or authority, that's fine.

A thornier question in large organisations, particularly if it is basically a one-person presentation, is this: what happens if the most senior member of staff is not nearly as good at presentation as one of the more junior people? My own view is that the better presenter must do the presentation, but that the superior should start off the proceedings with a brief introduction and end them with a short summary.

28

If the presentation is at all important, all the people making significant contributions should have understudies. Certainly the chief presenter must have one. The understudy's role is most important. The understudy:

- can provide an extra check on all the visual and stage management details;
- can discuss improvements with the presenter;
- often averts disaster on the day by spotting that something is missing from the dais or that the slides are out of order.

The knowledge that they will have to do it all themselves if illness strikes sharpens the understudies' observation and reactions wonderfully. (Shrewd presenters will complain to their understudy of slight headache and shivering the evening before the presentation.)

If you are in charge of the whole presentation, and especially if it is a large one, it is most unwise to take part in it yourself. Apart from the fact that you have quite enough to do already, there is another reason. Somebody must constantly be devising, amending, assessing and judging the presentation exclusively from the point of view of the audience. Anyone who is actually appearing in it will be at least partially preoccupied with their own performance and, moreover, their ego will make it impossible for them to be quite dispassionate about whether it's their piece that is the let-down point in the whole presentation.

Also, if you appear yourself it is harder to give helpful criticism and advice to the others – you and they will both have a sense that you are telling them they're not as good as you are. If this suspicion does not soften your criticism then it will harden their resistance: either way it will impair your effectiveness.

The final and most important principle in all the planning stages is this: never assume that the audience is going to be interested in the subject of your presentation. Expect them to be neutral – neither interested nor bored, but quite capable of being either. Unless you devote time and thought to the basic problem of keeping them interested, they can only too easily relapse into a boredom that is only a very short step from resentment.

29

Action checklist

1 Work through the draft presentation looking for places where interest drops.

2 Identify any explanations or arguments that are long or complicated and simplify them.

3 Consider ways of varying the texture of the presentation.

4 Be sure that any changes you have made to add interest are still relevant to your subject.

5 Keep sections short enough to maximise the audience's attention span.

6 Make sure each session ends on a high note.

7 Let the audience know what's coming up.

8 Get the audience involved.

9 Decide what you really want the audience to remember, and devise a way to make sure they will.

10 Decide who will deliver the presentation, giving the audience a varied but logical cast.

Thought-starters

1 *Think back over points and incidents you can remember from pre-sentations you have attended. What makes them memorable?*

2 *As a member of the audience, how far into a presentation do you usually get before you start to wonder when the next coffee break is due?*

3 *Do you find spoken presentations more interesting than writ-ten ones? If so, could you say why?*

4 *What was the last funny joke you heard at a presentation? Do you remember the point the speaker was making?*

5 *What do you think are the indicators that an audience's attention is beginning to wander?*

.**3**

The schedule

In a sense it is unnecessary to provide a schedule – it's fairly obvious what has to be done. Moreover, a great many presentations are arranged with less time than they need, and some have to be mounted at a day or two's notice and are extremely successful.

Nevertheless, I have found over the years that there are certain key meetings which need to be held, and if any of them are not held then the chances of success are noticeably reduced. A short and simple presentation with experienced presenters can combine some of these meetings, but the stages still have to be gone through. So it seemed best to list all the meetings which in an ideal world would take place before an important presentation. There are seven of them.

What shall we do?
■ ■ ■

This meeting is for the decisions listed at the beginning of Chapter 1: deciding on the purpose and aims of the presentation. When they are clear, this meeting should decide who should actually take part in the presentation and what the role of each should be. It is hard to say who should be at this meeting, but as a general rule you need at least three people – your basic presentation team:

- the person in charge of the presentation;
- an expert on the subject of the presentation – the product, plan, service etc. that is being presented (probably a presenter too);
- an expert on the object of the presentation, the needs, hopes and aspirations of the audience (probably a presenter too).

Action

Invite those who are required to take part in the presentation to the next meeting, with their understudies.

What shall we say?
■ ■ ■

(This meeting can be combined with the previous one – but all the stages still have to be worked through.) The basic team, and all other presenters and understudies, should attend. It is important at this stage to let everyone know how many more meetings there will be and what will be required of them at each stage, so that they don't try and jump straight to the end at once.

The presentation team briefs the presenters on the background, aims, approach and all practical details. They discuss with the presenters the general shape of the presentation, and the sort of thing each presenter should say and show. Each of the presenters should go off with a clear 'single sentence' in their mind of what the audience should be thinking at the end of their address.

Action

All presenters write out notes of what they propose to include in their address and send them in before the next meeting.

Briefing the presenters
■ ■ ■

We are now moving from Chapter 1 to Chapter 2. This is a full presentation team meeting again. It is an excellent idea, if at all possible, to invite to this meeting someone who will be in the audience, or at least someone who comes from the group being presented to, and reacts in the same way.

33

This meeting goes through the presenters' notes in order to:

- eliminate contradictions, overlapping points and duplication;
- see if there are any gaps which no one has covered;
- (most important) scrutinise all the proposed addresses from the point of view of the audience, so that the presenters can shorten sections that are well known, amplify the more interesting and unfamiliar, simplify or drop the too technical or detailed, avoid irritations, and be aware where they are most likely to encounter resistance or disbelief;
- build in the other general points about structuring the addresses for audience interest as described in Chapter 2.

The presenters should leave this meeting with a clear and accurate sense of the audience they will encounter.

> ## Action
>
> Presenters dictate (or write out – see Chapter 4) what they want to say, with strict instructions that, when delivered at normal pace, it will not go on for more than two-thirds of the speaking time allotted to them. They should send these drafts in before the next meeting, with ideas for visuals.

Production sessions

■ ■ ■

These are not full sessions. Ideally there should be a separate one for each presenter, along with the person running the presentation and at least one 'production manager', responsible for all slides, video, microphones, charts, and indeed all technical equipment and details of practical organisation.

34

Depending on your circumstances you may also need a graphic designer, camera operator or stills photographer, projectionist, stage designer, lighting expert and various other specialists. If the presentation is to be in a public building (cinema, theatre, hotel conference room etc.), a representative of their technical staff at these sessions can save a deal of trouble later.

This is the Chapter 2 meeting, where each address is studied for its impact and its dramatic, audience-holding qualities. Impact visuals are now discussed. All photographs, videos, OHPs, slides, charts, drawings, models, equipment and aids of every description are listed, and their design worked out.

> ## Action
>
> ■ *The presenter* must now finally turn the draft into a talk (see Chapter 4). But the transcript must not be turned into a paper; changes must be made on the basis of a 'spoken document'.
>
> ■ *The production manager* should set in motion the design and execution of all visual aids, and make sure that everything is completed and ready for the next meeting. (It never is, but you have to try.)

Except in the simplest of presentations there will usually be a gap of at least two weeks, and quite possibly four, between this meeting and the next.

The stagger-through
■ ■ ■

This stage has acquired the name stagger-through because run-through suggests a speed and smoothness which is a practical impossibility at this stage. This is the first bringing together of the presenters' final scripts, with all their visual material and aids, and an attempt to go through them in sequence.

Like the production sessions this should be done separately with each presenter. Now is the time to discover and correct errors in the execution of visuals, to come up against technical difficulties of lighting, movement and operation, and to time the script and make cuts if necessary. A stopwatch comes in handy at this stage.

35

Here too it helps tremendously if someone who will be in the audience can come along and comment, from the consumer's point of view. The next meeting will do, but this one gives more time for changes.

Action

Make any necessary corrections to visuals, sort out practical and technical snags, retime cut scripts and cut more if necessary.

The run-through
■ ■ ■

Everybody who has been involved in the presentation should come to this meeting. By now most of the practical and technical problems should be sorted out, and everyone can see for the first time something close to what the audience will see. Not much can now be done in the way of alterations and embellishments, but it is still possible to cut. It can be painful to do so this late, when so much care and trouble has been put in: nevertheless it is the ability to cut at this stage, even to cut a complete address, that sorts out the amateurs from the professionals.

Action

Tidy up any outstanding practical or technical problems, and make final cuts if necessary.

The dress rehearsal
■ ■ ■

This is different from the run-through in that it is held in the actual location where the presentation is to be given (if this is humanly possible), with all the attendant facilities and circumstances as close as possible to what they will be on the day. The purpose of this is to try and reveal any special snags that could not be foreseen, and to give the presenters some territorial familiarity to diminish their apprehensions.

If it is impossible to hold the dress rehearsal in the actual location it is still worth having a final run-through, incorporating any technical adjustments and cuts that may have been made at the last run-through. Even if there are none of these, it never hurts to hold a final run-through, the morning or day before the actual presentation if possible, if only for the added confidence it will give the presenters.

Action

Cross fingers.

Meeting	Who should attend	Action
What shall we do?	Person in charge of presentation Expert on subject Expert on audience	Invite participants to next meeting

What shall we say?	Basic team All other presenters Understudies	Presenters produce notes of address before next meeting
Briefing the presenters	Basic team All other presenters Understudies	Presenters produce scripts with ideas for visuals
Production session	Person in charge of presentation Production manager Presenters (individually)	Presenter turns draft into talk. Start preparing visuals
Stagger-through	Everyone	Make technical and practical adjustments – retime and cut if necessary
Run-through	Everyone	Technical fine-tuning and last-minute cuts
Dress rehearsal	Everyone	Cross fingers

37

Action checklist

1 Decide the purpose and aims of the presentation.

2 Decide who will do what.

3 Each presenter should work out a single sentence saying what they want to leave the audience thinking.

4 Presenters should each write notes for their session.

5 Notes should be checked to ensure they hold the audience's interest and cover all the necessary information.

6 Presenters dictate or write out what they want to say.

7 Study each section to decide on visuals and technical details.

8 Work through each section to identify problems and hiccups.

9 Run through the whole presentation in order. This is the last realistic chance to cut or alter.

10 Hold a dress rehearsal in the actual location (if possible).

Thought-starters

1 *How many mistakes in presentations you have attended can you remember? How many could have been avoided by better rehearsal?*

2 *What is the shortest time you have had in which to put together a presentation, and what is the longest? What were the benefits of each?*

3 *Think of the different types of visual aid you might use. How far in advance should you start preparing each type?*

4 *When you watch a presentation what are the signs that tell you how well planned and rehearsed it has been?*

5 *Have you ever been involved in a presentation that overran? Why did it happen? How could it have been avoided?*

4

Delivery and the use of words

Once we have established what we want to say, and in what order, we need to decide what words to say it with.

No matter how relevant the subject, and how interesting the format of the presentation, it is still perfectly possible to confuse the audience – even send them to sleep – merely through a poor choice of words and phrasing. So there is a handful of rules that need to be learnt at this stage. They're not difficult, but they are important.

The problems of unscripted presentation
■ ■ ■

Should the presenter have a written script, or just talk more or less spontaneously from a few notes? This is a constantly recurring question, and one to which more people come up with the wrong answer than any other.

To start with, let us all agree that the best talkers are those who are the most natural. They are easy, fluent, friendly, amusing and free from the fetters that seem to bind others to small pieces of paper. They are just talking to us in the most natural way in the world: no script for them – how could there be? They are talking only to us, and basing what they say on our reactions as they go along. Such a talk cannot, by definition, be scripted.

40

For most of us, however, that sort of performance is an aspiration rather than a description. Our tongues are not so honeyed, and our words are less winged. And even for those who can on occasions touch those heights, there are still three difficulties.

Visuals

A brilliant talker does not need visuals to stop the audience from falling asleep, but the subject of a presentation very often demands them. And, if you have them, it can be fatal to depart from the prepared order in which they are to appear. The slides, videos and flip charts are in a prearranged sequence, the operator has a fixed point at which to leave the slide machine and move across to the video-recorder, and a brilliant extempore performance will mess up the whole thing.

Time

A presentation is almost always limited in time, and a certain amount has to be said in that time. Without fairly careful scripting, time is likely to be wildly overrun, or important points omitted.

Finding the best way

If you accept that certain points have to be made in a certain time to a certain audience, the logic of optimisation takes over. There is a best order in which to make the points. There is a best way of putting them to make them clear to the audience. There are best words and phrases to emphasise your arguments. Quite soon you discover that any genuinely spontaneous performance is not practicable, so it might as well all be scripted.

Don't read them a paper
■ ■ ■

41

Most people decide they had better write down their presentation, and this is where it all goes wrong. They sit down at their desk, write out what they want to say, hand it to their secretary, and tell themselves that they have written their presentation. But they haven't. They have written a paper.

I am not sure why it should be slightly offensive and insulting to have a document read to you, or obviously memorised and recited at you, in this sort of situation. Eminent professors read papers to learned societies, and no one complains: but in that case the audience are usually receiving (or hope they are receiving) a privileged preview of a new contribution to knowledge which will later be published. I think it is partly because a presentation is usually felt to be to some extent a favour bestowed by those who attend on those who present. If it is all written out, why bother to make the journey and take up all this time? Why not just put the document in the post?

Reading or memorising the material is also an insult to the individuality of the audience: if they have taken the trouble to come along, they expect to be talked to as themselves, whereas a written document has obviously been completed before its author ever encountered them, and can equally obviously be delivered by any speaker to any audience. Indeed, the larger the audience, the less offensive it becomes (though it is never elegant): but when the audience is under a hundred, as most presentation audiences are, it can be sufficiently irritating to defeat the purpose of the presentation.

Certainly, the encyclopedia salesman who called on my wife and me one evening, and continued to recite his company's official spiel at us, word for word, as if he were chatting, gave the most powerful impression of fraudulent insincerity that I have ever witnessed in my own living room (at least when the television was off).

So it seems that if you read your script you are insulting, and if you learn it and recite it you are insincere. What is the answer?

42

Spoken English and written English
■ ■ ■

The answer lies in the difference between written and spoken English. If you write out a script and practise it enough, you will anyway have it pretty well by heart when the time comes; but if what you started from was written English, then it will still sound like a memorised document. If what you started from was spoken English, it will sound like an informal talk.

It is worth looking at the differences between the two kinds of language, because if only you can see the difference and avoid the pitfalls, it makes a tremendous improvement to your sense of ease and relaxation, and helps you to avoid the barrier which so many speakers unwittingly construct between themselves and their audience. What is more, it is perfectly possible to sit down at your desk and write spoken English – professional broadcasters do it all the time: you just have to be aware of what it involves.

I prefer to write out the whole presentation. After all (and especially if time is limited), there is always a best way of putting something – best argument, best order, best phrase – and you are more likely to think it up and work it out by making yourself write it down in advance than by thinking on your feet. So how do you stop it sounding like a recitation?

Writing spoken English

First of all, the spoken language has its roots not in literature or newspapers but in the unselfconscious speech of ordinary people. When writing written English you ask yourself if what you have put is clear, grammatical and concise, but with spoken English it has to go through another filter as well: is it the sort of thing someone might actually say to someone else? Or, to be more precise, is there anything in it that no one could possibly say to anyone else?

On the printed page you may get away with all sorts of things that you simply can't say in everyday speech:

43

In speech a group of three is not a, b and c, but a and b and c. Anything that smacks of journalese or archaism or purple prose or literariness is a bar to communication – as a member of the audience you instantly feel 'whoever this person is talking to, it isn't me'. This doesn't mean that everything has to be at the level of chit-chat on the contrary, part of the craft consists in writing carefully and well, while the audience just feel they are being talked to by an interesting person.

In fact, writing good, spoken English may mean writing ungrammatically. Grammatically correct English can be bad spoken English; just count how many times anyone says the word 'whom' to you tomorrow. Very few people can say it and get away with it.

The spoken version may be bad grammar, but in a presentation it's the only way. And, of course, you can cash in on the vernacular, and make your point a good deal more vigorously:

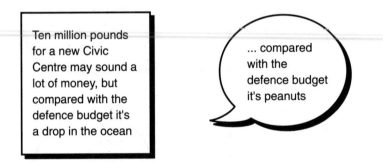

Slang always gets a licence to operate in the vernacular long before it's allowed out on the printed page solo, without the L-plates of inverted commas.

And with spoken English you can use the first and second person where the more formal written English would use the third:

> The user will have encountered similar examples of failures of domestic equipment which can be exasperating even if not dangerous

> I expect you know the sort of thing I mean – the gadget that wakes you up with a hot cup of tea at three in the morning, the vacuum cleaner that blows when it ought to suck. Even when it's harmless it's the kind of thing that drives me up the wall – and it's not always harmless

Incidentally, no respectable writer of written English would put 'sort of thing' and 'kind of thing' so close to each other on a printed page, but in spoken English it passes unnoticed.

45

Using spoken English

There is another principle of spoken English which is also true of written English, but even more important with an audience which cannot stop and puzzle a sentence out: avoid abstract nouns. They are the barbiturates of communication: soporific in small doses and lethal in large ones. A steady and sober citizen who will tell you privately 'We'll make sure you can hear it properly' will write 'we will give special attention to the provision of adequate sound reception facilities'. Some people seem to be drawn magnetically to using abstract nouns in writing that they would never dream of saying.

> The consequence of your interposition of a manual obstruction on my area of locution is the inhibition of communication

> If you put your hand over my mouth I can't talk

A total ban on the use of abstract nouns, despite the restrictions it imposes, would have made a net overall improvement to nearly all the presentations I have ever attended. The aim of all writing, according to Robert Louis Stevenson, is to affect your reader precisely as you wish. This is equally true of writing spoken English, and the word 'precisely' is the key: the concrete noun is a precision tool, the abstract noun a blunt instrument.

Another vital rule of good spoken English is to use short words and short sentences. Do not say: 'Circumstances occasionally arise involving a situation in which one or more of the contributing personnel wishes to exercise the option of continuing in employment beyond the normal retirement date as specified in their formal contractual agreement, in which eventuality suitable arrangements can be concluded for the further maintenance of contribution and consequent enhancement of eventual benefit.' Just say: 'Sometimes people want to stay on after they're sixty. If so they can still stay in the pension scheme.'

Apart from that, there are a few other useful guidelines to keep in mind when you are choosing which words to use:

- use active rather than passive verbs; eg 'we need your help' rather than 'your help is needed by us' and 'safety helmets save lives' rather than 'lives are saved by safety helmets';
- avoid technical terms unless you *know* the audience is familiar with them;
- always use your own words and phrases, the sort you actually use in conversation;
- cut out jargon ruthlessly.

Jargon can confuse an audience faster than almost anything. I have seen computer people quite unaware of the effect they had on lay audiences by talking blithely about 'redundancy' and 'graceful degradation' with their special data-processing meanings of which the listeners were wholly unaware.

So much for the first and great difference between the two kinds of English. The source is the spoken language, not the

46

written language, and you must never make yourself say anything that would sound oddly formal, stilted or literary if used in ordinary conversation. Incidentally, you also have to be careful with words that sound the same – remember that size may mean stature or it may mean windy suspirations and the audience haven't got the spelling to help them.

Word order

The second fundamental difference is that when reading the written word you can go at your own pace; you can pause to reflect, or to consult a dictionary or Fowler's *Modern English Usage*, or you can go back and read the beginning of the sentence or chapter or article again. If it is written in such a way that you are obliged to do this it is probably not very well written, but you can make it out in the end.

47

The spoken word, however, comes at you down a single line, as it were. You can never look on to the end of a sentence or back to the start of it.

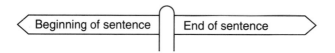

You can't put it on pause for a second.

You can't make it go more slowly.

And so in writing for that sort of communication you have to think in a new way about clarity and lucidity: in a presentation you not only have to present all the relevant information clearly, you also have to present it in the best order for instant assimilation.

For instance, if you say 'Dickens, Socrates, Drake, Lincoln, Henry VIII – they all had beards', you don't know why all the names are being mentioned until the last word of the sentence. When it comes you are asking the audience to go back and mentally draw beards on all five of them – if they can remember who they were.

48

If you say 'Dickens had a beard, and so did Socrates, Drake, Lincoln and Henry VIII' you are drawing the beards on all the time. I'm not saying you can't ask them to make this mental effort, only that you must be aware you are demanding it.

Similarly, if someone tells you 'In the last year Harry Smith has climbed the Matterhorn, swum the Hellespont, crossed the Sahara, run from London to Brighton, shot the Niagara Falls in a canoe, and all this blindfold and with one hand tied behind his back', they may get a certain shock effect, but they are asking you to go back and do all those things again in your head in the light of this new information.

You also have to be very careful with the involved sentence culminating in the main verb. It is supposed to be bad literary style to write a sentence that has various grammatical ending places before the full stop – the sort of sentence where you can go on chopping pieces off the end without necessitating syntactic change. But it's usually good spoken English writing, for two reasons.

Read this literary version: 'Whatever the works manager says, if the financial projections look right and the market tests are encouraging, at least in the capital goods business, it's usually safe to authorise a development budget.' In the first place you have to store all those parentheses in your head until you know what the speaker and the works manager were arguing about; in the second place this is the opposite of how people talk.

In ordinary speech the main thoughts nearly always come first, or near the front. 'Whatever the works manager says, it's usually safe to authorise a development budget, at least in the capital goods business, as long as the financial projections look right and the market tests are encouraging.' So, on the whole, it's better to put your parentheses after the main verb, and usually a bad idea to pile several up before it.

Signposting

Also, the audience has no paragraphing to guide them; you must allow for this too. The device to use is known as 'signposting'. The problem is that you know perfectly well where you have got to in your presentation, and where you are going: the audience does not, and they cannot see your notes, nor can they glance forward as they can with a book or a report to see what is coming. It is therefore important to provide them with the equivalent of a paragraph.

This only needs a summarising sentence to round off one section, followed by an introductory statement or question to introduce the next. 'Right. So we've seen that our present warehouse capacity will be insufficient when we open our northern region branches. So, what do we do? Well, we have narrowed the practical options down to three, and I'll describe them briefly first and then discuss them in turn. Option one is ...' Good paragraphing is a great help to retention, since you are supplying the audience not only with information but also with a ready-made filing system to put it in. Signposting is a tremendous aid to clarity. Had Hamlet been giving a presentation rather than talking to himself, you can see how he might have employed it.

To be or not to be – that is the question;

> Well, that's the basic question, so now we'll take a more detailed look at the viable options.

Whether 'tis nobler in the mind to suffer
The slings and arrows of outrageous fortune
Or to take arms against a sea of troubles
And by opposing end them. To die, to sleep –

> Of course, sleep cuts both ways; so I'll breifly outline its main benefits, and then its chief disadvantages.

No more – and by a sleep to say we end
The heartache and the thousand natural shocks
That flesh is heir to. 'Tis a consummation
Devoutly to be wished. To die, to sleep –

> And the down side ...

To sleep – perchance to dream. Ay, there's the rub.
For in that sleep of death what dreams may come
When we have shuffled off this mortal coil
Must give us pause.

> It might be useful at this point to take a quick look at why people so rarely choose death ...

True, it doesn't actually do wonders for the poetry or the drama, but it certainly clarifies the argument.

Plant your facts

One invaluable device for signposting is the rhetorical question. We used it in the previous paragraph: 'Our present warehouse capacity will be insufficient. So what do we do? Well ...' It also has an important function in arranging the order in which you present your information. You must have noticed that it's much easier to assimilate a fact if you wanted to know it than if it's just presented to you. The rhetorical question is a good way of digging a hole to plant a fact in.

I first learnt this by seeing it done the wrong way on television. There was a film reconstructing Hannibal's route across the Alps. The commentary said 'That flat rock is probably where Hannibal spent the third night, because Livy says they only made five miles on the third day and Polybius says they camped on a high, flat rock.'

How much better to say, 'Now we had to work out where they spent the third night. Well, it must have been near here because Livy says they only made five miles on the third day. Polybius said it was on a high, flat rock.' By that time everyone is looking for the rock anyway, and they will probably spot it first.

Use of examples and analogy

Perhaps this is also the point at which to advocate the use of analogy. A well-chosen parallel from within the audience's experience often saves a hundred pounds' worth of visual aids or ten minutes of involved explanation. I only started to understand what computer software was when someone produced this analogy:

'Compare software with secretaries. Their value depends on three factors: (a) their general intelligence and suitability for the job; (b) their training – maths, English, languages, shorthand, typing, book-keeping and so on; (c) how well they know and carry out the specific jobs of your office and your organisation.

'Well, in terms of computers: (a) is the basic design and circuitry of the computer – like intelligence there's not much you can do about it now; (b) is the basic operating system, supplied with the computer, and the standard software – functions like spreadsheets and invoicing which nearly every user wants from a computer, just as they want shorthand and typing from a secretary; (c) is the user's own software, the programmes special to their own company which they write for themselves, just as you teach secretaries their duties when they join.'

That sort of simple and homely parallel may not be a complete explanation, but it is clear and brief, and ideal for a presentation: if anyone wants to know more, there are lots of books available.

So much for the two main ways in which a presentation script differs from a written paper: it draws on the vocabulary, grammar and syntax of ordinary speech instead of literary English, and it comes at the viewer down a single line; they can't see what's coming or what's gone, or vary the pace, or go back. Also, I ought to make it clear that the principles of good writing still hold for good speaking: compression, lucidity, vividness, force, avoiding ambiguity – these are the aims of a presentation script just as much as for writing for the printed page. It is the means of achieving these aims that are different.

Different levels of knowledge
■ ■ ■

There is one other difference that matters as well: difference in level of knowledge. Some of your audience are specialist experts, some are reasonably well informed, some are rather hazy about it all. If you were writing a journal this wouldn't matter: some would read it fast, some slowly, some would just glance at it. No one would blame you for putting in something they already knew – they bought the journal and it's their fault if it's too technical, or if there's nothing they want to know in it. But, especially if you invited them to the presentation, do you explain things carefully for the less expert and bore or even insult the specialists, or do you talk to the experts and baffle the non-specialists (who may be senior to them)?

This, in fact, is a problem that broadcasters face in an acute form. Suppose, for instance, you are writing about why Churchill lost the 1945 general election, and suppose you suspect many of your audience will be quite young and won't know the background. Do you say, 'Churchill was leader of the Conservative party. He had led a coalition government for most of the Second World War. Until war broke out he had spent ten years in parliament without senior office, having been Chancellor of the Exchequer before that'? If you do, half the audience will decide this is too elementary and so not meant for them.

53

In fact, of course, you have to use dodges. You say, ' How do you pigeonhole a man who held a post as senior as Chancellor of the Exchequer, then disappeared from the political scene almost completely for ten years, and within a few months of returning to it was prime minister of a coalition government, leading the nation to victory in the Second World War?'

You have to find all the possible ways of dropping background facts casually and inoffensively. And there is a wealth of invaluable phrases you can employ frequently:

- 'broadly speaking';
- 'for the most part';
- 'in general';
- 'with certain exceptions'.

All of these help you to avoid piling up tedious exceptions and qualifications while showing the experts you know about them. Of course, if you are worried about short-changing the experts you can make up for it by typing up all the details and distributing them afterwards (not before, or they will be reading while you are talking). You will, of course, tell the experts that the details are in the supporting documentation.

Alternatively (or additionally) you can bring an expert colleague with you to make a technical presentation just for the experts, or answer technical questions when the main presentation is over.

You will also find that specialist experts will not object to a really good explanation or analogy – they may want to use it themselves one day. But you have to remember both halves of C.P. Scott's advice:

> 'Never overestimate your audience's knowledge;
> never underestimate their intelligence.'

54

It is fatal to believe your audience is less intelligent than you, though wise to expect them to be less well informed.

Delivery
■ ■ ■

The actual delivery of the presentation, elocution, voice production and projection is not something you can teach in a book: moreover, since microphones are virtually standard for larger presentations it is much less of a critical factor than it used to be. But certain points are still worth looking out for.

For most presenters, the chief problem is to overcome the speaker's rigidity: you must often have seen how someone who talks in an animated, interested and persuasive way suddenly becomes wooden and monotonous when they step out on to a platform to address a couple of dozen people. Some terrible demon of self-consciousness seems to paralyse the muscles of their face and constrict their vocal chords. All I can say is that experience makes this demon depart, but the departure can be delayed by two factors:

1 using written English instead of spoken English (see above);

2 failure to realise that good speaking consists of addressing a large number of people as if they were a single person.

The aim, in fact, is to talk in the same way as you would talk to a couple of friends over a drink. Try to keep your manner the same:

- movements of face, head and body;
- range of vocal pitch and volume;
- gestures;
- pace;
- pauses.

But it is not a question of acquiring these characteristics; the task is to remove the barriers which are keeping them back – learning to remove the inhibitions that stop you being your normal, natural, friendly self once you get up on your feet. Anyone who cannot remove them with practice and experience should give up speaking in public, or take a public-speaking course.

55

However, if you are addressing a thousand people without a microphone, this natural and easy manner is impossible, and you are in the world of genuine oratory which is something quite different in technique, even if identical in objective – see Chapter 7.

Technique and mannerisms
■ ■ ■

Presenters can help each other by watching one another for a few common and obvious faults which are hard to notice in oneself, and commenting, encouragingly and constructively, on each other's performance. You can learn quite a lot just by watching other people doing it wrong and discussing why. These are the chief technical faults to watch out for.

Mumbling

It's better to be too loud than too quiet.

Hesitancy

Excessive pauses, usually filled with '... er ...'. Almost always a sign of insufficient rehearsal.

Gabbling

Much rarer, and easy to correct once you know you are doing it.

Catch phrases

'The point is ...', 'and all that sort of thing ...', 'if you know what I mean ...'. These phrases are harmless in themselves, but if they become a frequent verbal mannerism they can distract the audience. These mannerisms are only worth worrying about if they are a real distraction. You can sometimes do more harm by drawing people's attention to an unconscious mannerism than by leaving it alone.

Poor eye-contact

Do not move your gaze from the floor to the ceiling via the back wall. Look at people – not aggressively or hypnotically, just look at them as you do in normal conversation. And that means all of them, including those at the sides. Also be aware that if you turn away or look down the audience is more likely to lose what you are saying.

Mannerisms

Physical mannerisms, such as scratching the ear and so on, are only worth correcting if they are frequent enough to distract the audience so that they are watching for it with more interest than they are giving to the presentation.

Dropping the voice

The most common fault of amateur speakers is to drop the voice at the end of each sentence. Those who do this are usually completely unconscious of it, and it has a most boring and deadening effect, since it makes it seem that the talk has ended with each sentence, and it has to be started off again each time. However, once the offenders are made aware that they are doing it – by listening to a recording of themselves, for instance – they are already three-quarters of the way to overcoming it.

Action checklist

1 Don't sacrifice comfortable idiomatic phrasing in favour of good grammar – use the vernacular.

2 If you can, replace the third person with the first or second person.

3 As a rule, keep the main point of the sentence near the beginning.

4 Signpost your presentation by 'paragraphing' it for your audience.

5 Use rhetorical questions to plant your facts.

6 Avoid abstract nouns wherever you can.

7 Use examples whenever possible.

8 Allow for different levels of knowledge in your audience.

9 Address the audience as if it were a single person.

10 Avoid repetitive verbal and physical mannerisms.

Thought-starters

1 *Do the presenters you most enjoy listening to work from scripts, or notes, or do they just speak spontaneously?*

2 *Have you ever read one of your own scripts aloud and noticed yourself trying to use a phrase that you can't say comfortably?*

3 *Who is your favourite public speaker? Could you say why?*

4 *Have you ever sat through a long explanation of something you already knew at a presentation? How did you feel?*

5 *If you open the nearest book at random, could you rewrite the first paragraph you see for a listener rather than a reader?*

Note to Chapter 4

As an example of the difference between written and spoken English, I have made up a paragraph of the sort one encounters all too frequently in management papers, and 'translated' it into the sort of language I would use if I were delivering it in a speech or presentation. It is no accident that the spoken version is longer – the vague abstractions of the written version have to be solidified into concrete examples if they are to penetrate the audience's mind through the ear instead of the eye.

Written English

The reader may have noted the tendency to inflation of self-importance on the part of the scientist and development engineer in large organisations. It is the product of a combination of influences – partly the significance accorded to their contribution in the area of their industrial operations, partly a recognition of the distinction accorded to their qualifications in their social and domestic environment. Furthermore, their section of the population is given particular prominence in the achievement of the objectives of the nation.

There is also the opportunity for building a reputation among professional and academic institutions outside the organisation, both in the national and the international fields. In addition there is the enhancement of the attitude of engineers and scientists as an exception, produced by those with responsibility for the management of the organisation: their nonconformity, unreliability and intellectual capacity become the subject of others' respect and admiration, despite its divergence from their own conscientious normality of behaviour.

Consequently, the occupations are full of temptation towards an arrogant inflation of their own self-esteem.

Spoken English

"Let's imagine a large research and development organisation. Suppose it has a hundred scientists working in it – or say two hundred if you like. And imagine you're one of those scientists – perhaps a development engineer. Quite soon you begin to feel that if an organisation that big hinges on you, you must be quite someone. And you begin to feel you ought to be treated as quite someone too. After all, you're pretty well respected at home; the neighbours tell visitors that you're 'a scientist' in a reverent sort of voice – the voice their parents would have used to say 'He's a priest'. And you've even got a sort of national importance: don't people in government keep saying how we need more scientists if the economy is to grow?

But that's not all. You have an existence, an identity, in a world beyond the organisation. You've got links with your old university, and with other universities. You attend scientific congresses, not just at home but abroad as well. You belong to a fellowship that's far wider and far more illustrious than the grey organisation staff who work alongside you. And, what's more, they go out of their way to help you feel you're an exception They build your myth. They invent stories about your absent-mindedness. They tell each other how you corrected the computer's square roots. Of course they're all sober-suited and clean shaven, and yet if you arrive in a yellow shirt with no jacket and a beard, they're delighted.

One way and another, if you're a scientist in industry today it's quite a struggle *not* to think of yourself as a cut above everyone else.**"**

59

.5

Visual aids and the use of pictures

To list all the available visual aids on the market, with their full details and variations, to describe the operation, and assess the advantages and disadvantages of each one, deserves several volumes. This chapter deals only with those which are most handy for presentations, and is concerned not with the routine uses which most people get right, but with the ways in which I have most often seen them misused, messed up or wasted.

The purpose of this chapter is to look at the practical opportunities and pitfalls of visual aids; Chapter 6 deals with their design.

Commonly used visual aids
■ ■ ■

Most of the visual aids in common use offer presenters opportunities which they fail to take, and they all have special ways of tripping them up. The following list gives you the main points to watch.

Prepared flip charts

These pre-prepared visual aids are very useful and are not used enough.

- Chief fault is that drawings can be too small for audience to see detail. Must be bold and simple.

- Very good (and not sufficiently used) for cartoon illustrations of abstract concepts like 'inattention' (someone reading a newspaper while about to walk into a manhole) or 'accuracy' (an arrow hitting a bullseye).

- It can be distracting if a picture is left up after it has served its purpose, but if you fold back to the cover each time you may have trouble finding your place. The answer is to have a neutral interleaf after every picture or picture sequence (it doesn't have to be a blank – it can be a symbol, a company logo, or a simple picture that is relevant to your whole presentation).

Flip charts

Flip charts are very useful if you have any audience participation sessions in your presentation: they are the single,
most useful visual aid for training. However, for most structured presentations you will know in advance what points
you want to make and how you want to illustrate them. If
this is the case it saves time (at the presentation), and avoids
a lot of potential pitfalls, if you use a prepared flip chart. But
for those times when you want to leave room for the spon-
taneity that can be generated by audience participation, here
are some guidelines.

63

- Colours are much more effective used on white than on
  coloured paper. Remember that some colours show up
  better than others – it's a good idea to get someone to
  stand at the back of the room while you're rehearsing
  to make sure they can see everything clearly.

- If you are right-handed, the flip chart should be on
  your left as you face the audience, so you obscure much
  less of it when drawing. If you have room, start drawing one-third of the way across, using only the far
  two-thirds, and you will obscure less still.

- When pointing at the flip chart, stay on the same side and point with your left hand, so that you stay facing the audience.

- If you have to talk while writing or drawing, remember that by turning round you have suddenly made it twice as hard for the audience to hear you. Better to avoid doing so – or at least avoid confiding in the flip chart.

- To make it easier to avoid talking while writing or drawing: try and plan your use of the flip chart so that you are never using it for more than a few seconds at a stretch. Even if you only break off for a sentence or two, it's a great deal better.

- Because you can't erase everything, you have to get rid of the previous sheet each time. If the sheets fold back at the top, they are liable to start falling back on you after the first six. One answer to this is to have a large bulldog clip with which to hold them back. If they are perforated and you just tear them off and drop them, the stage starts to look ridiculous by about sheet six, as well as being a slight embarrassment to those who follow. Or will you go down on your hands and knees and pick up the fallen sheets yourself? A decent-sized cardboard box is usually the answer. But the moral is clear: rehearse right through.

- Good straight lines, circles etc. can be achieved by drawing them on the board in pencil before the presentation, then inking over the pencil line. Audience can't see your pencil line and thinks you are another Leonardo da Vinci.

- Keep a spare pen in your pocket.

- Check the flip chart in advance for stability (I would be ashamed to mention anything this elementary if I had not witnessed the consequence of a failure to do so).

Whiteboards

Much like the flip chart in principle, and most of the same rules apply. It does have a particular disadvantage, though, that you need to wipe out material in order to produce new information. There are one or two additional points worth making:

- use non-permanent rather than permanent marker pens;
- a dry duster is nothing like so efficient as a damp duster or sponge;
- clear the board as soon as you have finished with what is on it. It's a distraction if you leave up old drawings when you've moved on.

Overhead projector (OHP)

By OHP I mean the sort operated by the presenter. There are two ways of using overhead projectors; one is to prepare the slides in advance, and the other is to write or draw on them during the presentation, as an alternative to using a flip chart.

OHPs can be tricky to use as they can take the presenters' attention away from the audience. They have to worry about getting the transparencies in the right order, getting them the right way up and the right way round, they have to keep checking the screen behind them, and the effect can often be cumbersome, didactic and slow.

There is really no advantage at all in using OHP transparencies in place of flip charts, to write or draw on as you go
along, except at very large presentations where a flip chart is
too small to be seen from the back, and you can get a larger,
and higher, throw from an OHP.

Prepared OHP graphics are very easy to generate on a computer and copy on to acetate, and can be very effective. They
are cheaper and easier to produce than slides, and the projector itself is less complicated and likely to break down than a
slide projector (but not so reliable that you don't need to check
it thoroughly all the same).

Along with slides, OHPs are the easiest visual aids to misuse
through bad design, and the next chapter deals with the pitfalls to avoid when designing them. But from a practical
point of view, there are several points that need to be made.

- Do not switch the light on until the slide is in position,
  and switch it off before you move the slide away.

- Rehearse thoroughly so you know exactly where to put
  your hand on each new slide, and where you're putting
  the ones you've finished with.

- Make sure you position the OHP projector on the stage
  in such a way that it does not have to be moved until
  the last presenter has finished with it, otherwise a lot
  of time (and credibility) will be wasted while the presenter tries to line it up again. For this reason you

should make sure before you start that it is not placed so prominently as to be a permanent distraction to the audience, and that it does not mask their view of the presenters, the screen, or any of the other visual aids.

■ Line up the OHP projector before you start the presentation, and rehearse with it until you *know* it is in the right position. The first time you turn it on you can allow yourself a cursory glance to check that no one has disturbed it in the interim, but do not then keep looking at it nervously every time you change the picture. You should become so familiar with the equipment that you can use it casually.

■ Make sure the lighting for the presentation is not so strong that it bleaches out the OHPs. Rehearsal in the location will establish this; if it is a problem you can either reduce the level of lighting on the stage or arrange for someone to turn the lights off while the projector is being used. In this case, you will need to make sure there is still some light shining on the presenter.

67

■ If using a pointer, don't let the point wander vaguely round the screen. Point at what you want, leave it there motionless, then take it away.

■ If using a pointer, suppress all impulses to use it as a swagger stick, conductor's baton, backscratcher, seven-iron or toothpick.

Slides

Of all the available visual aids, I can think of none that are used more ineptly than slides. They are very valuable but can be great destroyers of presentations. Give slide projectors the care and respect you would give a loaded pistol. The faults are of two kinds, conceptual and operational. By conceptual faults I mean inadequate thought about design, which is what Chapter 6 is about.

Faults in design and content are all barriers to communication. There are however plenty of operational faults you can make, which provoke something much more damaging – ridicule. When the third slide comes on upside down, even the most polite audience is starting to laugh. After the fifth, there isn't a dry seat in the house. However much people may sympathise, each of them takes away a private conviction that you're not to be trusted with hanging up a picture, let alone carrying out a £5 million aerospace contract.

Most of the problems centre on either the projector or the projectionist.

The projector

Consider the manufacturer's problem. The machine is electrical in power, mechanical in operation, and hot all the time it is running. It must be light and portable, but strong and resistant to bangs, bashes and dropping on the floor. It must be easily operated even by buffoons. Purchasers expect it to be cheap and to run efficiently, and without maintenance, for upwards of thirty-five years.

Now read the preceding paragraph again.

Right? Then I hope you have made the necessary deduction. *You must assume the projector is going to go wrong.* In fact, I am constantly surprised that they do not go wrong more often, but they go wrong enough. It is not disastrous if you are prepared for it (standby projector, vital pictures also on flip chart, contingency plans throughout), but if you have assumed that the projector will not go wrong and also hinged your presentation on it, you deserve all you get.

Always try out all the slides in advance on the projector you will actually be using, if possible in the place where you will be using it. Your slides may be the wrong size or the heat of the projector may burn them – you never know till you try.

The projectionist

You may have one of those projectors which you operate yourself by pressing a button. They have a great advantage, which is unified control. You yourself load the slides, you yourself project them. But if you are using a machine that requires a separate projectionist then you are up against the problem of divided control.

If you think the task of slide projectionist is another technical job like house electrician, I have to assume that you have never given a presentation that included a slide sequence. Technical proficiency is only a very small part of the job. It chiefly requires intellect, initiative, coolness of head and presence of mind.

69

GOOD PROJECTIONISTS

- They must have a thorough knowledge of, and familiarity with, the script.

- They must be alert for every accidental change of order, and be ready to rearrange their slides accordingly.

- They must be incapable of confusing the signal 'next slide' with the signal 'remove this slide'.

- They must never, of course, put a slide inside out or upside down, and never knock the next trayload on to the floor as they are about to reload.

For all these reasons the presenter's understudy, if there is one, is the person to operate the projector (projectionists themselves should also have understudies). But whoever it is, I would suggest the following procedure:

- they should go through the slides by hand against the script and then, having loaded them, go through them with the script twice;

- they must never make any cuts or order changes after their final rehearsal;

- they should try and avoid reloads during the presentation (use a second cassette or a second projector);

- if a slide is required twice they should make two copies, never try to lift it out and insert it in a different place;

- the projectionist must have a torch to find fallen slides under seats;

- they should agree a breakdown procedure, e.g. if a slide sticks do they drop it or try and return to it?

70

Lighting

If you have prepared and rehearsed sufficiently, then three-quarters of the practical problems of using slides in a presentation have been taken care of. The one remaining important question that affects the actual performance is lighting.

Beyond doubt the best answer is to have a spotlight on the speaker and no other light in the room except for the slide projector. This, however, can look a bit silly if you only have one or two slides in a thirty-minute presentation. You may find the slides can be grouped into one or two continuous sequences, so you can have someone put the lights on or off, or you may prefer to have low general lighting and try to avoid allowing too much light to spill on the screen.

There are various compromises, and the main point is to think about them in advance, but if you are going to have lighting changes during the presentation then make someone other than the projectionist responsible for them.

The performance

Apart from the guidelines above, there are just six principal errors to watch out for.

- It is quite astonishing how often presenters put a slide on and take it off again without referring to it or even apparently noticing it – even if the slide is quite complex and needs explaining. Unless the slide is instantly and totally intelligible it must be referred to, perhaps explained and possibly talked through, with sufficient pause for the audience to take it in.

- Never stand between any member of the audience and the screen. Above all, never stand between the projector and the screen, not just because of the shadow you cast but also because the part of the slide projected on to your face makes you look silly and completely distracts the audience.

- Do not keep looking over your shoulder at every slide change just to see if the right one has come up. You must *know* it has, which is what rehearsal is all about. You will, of course, frequently look at the slide with the audience when talking about some actual detail on it.

71

- The moment you turn towards the screen you make it extremely hard for the audience to hear what you are saying. Better to stand square to the audience with the screen beside you (on your right if you are right-handed), and turn towards it with your head and shoulders only.

- Once a slide has made its point it should be removed unless there is a positive reason for keeping it there.

- As with OHPs, the wandering pointer is a fruitful source of distraction. If you have to use one (and don't unless you can't reach places you have to indicate) then place it straight on the spot you are referring to, keep it still, and take it away as soon as you have finished.

One final point: you may be provided with a powerful torch whose beam projects a small bright arrow on to the screen to identify points on slides. *Do not use it*. It is nearly always a distraction, both to the speaker who has to aim it and find the target, and to the audience as it wanders around the screen like Tinkerbell in *Peter Pan*.

This torch does have a use, but a highly specialised one: it is useful for identifying obscure details in actuality slides (landscapes, X-rays, news photographs) when the screen is too large or too distant to use a pointer. Any slide you design yourself should be designed to be clear without it, and with nearly all others you will be able to identify details quite satisfactorily either verbally or with a pointer.

Build-up visuals

This includes all those visual aids like magnetic boards, slot boards, pin boards etc., where you build up a picture by adding to a basic design as you go along. The simplest and cheapest form, which used to be used by the army, is a set of cards backed with sandpaper, placed on a blanket stretched over a blackboard. It works surprisingly well.

The snag lies in confusion over pieces to be added. If you are adding on six different types of visual design, and you have ten of each, you spend most of the presentation hunting through sixty assorted objects for the one you want. The rule must be to use either a very limited number or a very limited range.

The alternative (which gets over this problem) is the revelation board, which starts blank or with a simple framework and is progressively revealed by removing blank cards (it is of course the same basic piece of equipment, but used for subtraction instead of addition).

The snag here is revealing too slowly in the early stages, so that boredom sets in because the audience can see how much further there is to go. You must use the stripper's technique of removing the first coverings fairly quickly: as interest rises you can afford to slow down a little and draw out the suspense.

If all these warnings are heeded and all the precautions are taken, slides alone can turn a pedestrian talk into a competent presentation. But they can also turn a man into a monkey.

Physical objects

73

In the search for helpful or memorable visuals, it is all too easy to forget the value of a small object fished out of the pocket, or a larger one from under the desk. It is worth making a special note to think if there is any object, or part of an object, which could be interesting and reasonably relevant to display. Because the presenters are familiar with the inside of a video-recorder, for example, they forget that their audience has quite possibly never seen one.

Simply producing something and holding it up lifts the presentation for several reasons:

- it turns an abstract idea into a physical object;
- it causes virtually no delay;
- it substitutes a memorable picture for a forgettable word.

If you have enough objects to pass round the audience, better still.

One of the most memorable uses of solid objects in this way was demonstrated in England just after transistors had been developed. British engineers and physicists were desperately and fruitlessly trying to get hold of them for examination and experiment when an American came over to address a learned society about them. At one stage he said 'Anybody want to take one home?', and to a disbelieving gasp he fished in his pocket and brought out a great handful of transistors, and just threw them into the audience.

The effect, I am told, was like throwing a handful of rice to a crowd of starving refugees. Distinguished professors grovelled and fought on their hands and knees, there was pushing and clawing and stamping on fingers and cries of accusation and pain, and it was minutes before the flushed and flustered gathering returned to their seats clutching their booty. Only then did the lecturer say, 'It's all right, they're all duds'.

74

Working models

The successful use of a working model is usually the high point of a presentation – ask any science teacher. If it fails to work, it is almost always a major disaster. This, however, is not an argument against the use of working demonstrations, only a plea for the most extreme care in preparation and rehearsal, and also (where possible) a standby that has been equally well tested and prepared.

Those who are to participate in the demonstration should practise and practise until boredom sets in, and for this almost more than anything else the actual location for the presentation should be checked for power supply, ventilation, fire regulations or anything else that could throw everything out at the last minute.

Tape-recordings

Aural rather than visual aids. They are not often called on, but it is worth thinking if there isn't some noise or music or spontaneous dialogue that might help. But it can be offensive to use tape-recordings of messages from members of your own organisation who might have come in person. There are one or two things you need to be aware of if you are using tape-recordings.

75

- There are a lot of pieces of working equipment that can go wrong – speakers, plugs and connections, the tape player, the tape etc. Make sure you check and double check your equipment, and still have a fallback in case it goes wrong 'on the night'.

- Tape-to-tape machines sometimes have a feature which is very useful if you have several separate sound cues in your presentation: an automatic stop. You simply insert a section of clear tape between each cue, and the machine will automatically stop at the end of one piece, and be lined up to start in the right place when you press the play button for the next cue. This means that nobody has to stand over the tape player to switch it off each time. But be careful: I have known a tape-to-tape player quietly go past an automatic stop when no one was looking (the speakers had been turned down) – and trying to find the right place to start the next cue when you haven't rehearsed it because you didn't know you needed to is no easy task. The rule is: never assume the equipment will work.

■ Always set the sound levels on the speakers in advance, and be aware that a roomful of people absorbs a great deal of sound, so you need to set the levels slightly on the high side. Be prepared for the fact that if you turn the volume up too high the sound will distort. Don't wait until five minutes before the presentation starts to find this out.

Video

A good video is the surest and most complete presentation in itself. However, a video made for a different purpose, but included in your presentation, needs special care.

■ Be careful not to run any section for too long. After a while it starts to take over and become the presentation, diminishing the importance and impact of everything else.

■ Resist the temptation to use a good piece of video just because it's good. Discipline yourself to reject it unless you can make it relevant. People remember good video, and you don't want their most vivid memory to be of something irrelevant.

- Remember that video is for *moving* pictures; it is to show things that move. Don't commission a video when still pictures would do the job better as well as more cheaply.

- Space your video sections carefully throughout the presentation for maximum effect.

- Be very careful of commenting live over silent pictures. Once the video has started it is more or less inexorable: if you have a sneezing fit, the pictures will go on changing at the same rate (unlike slides). You may get behind and be unable to catch up or find your place. If you do decide to risk it, at least have plenty of rehearsal with the picture and get to know it well, with special attention to the points at which the picture is about to change to something else: otherwise you find yourself talking about a picture that is not there, and failing to explain one that is.

77

- If you have an audience of more than about fifteen people a standard television screen will be too small, and you will be better off using a video projector. These are about the same size as a normal video player, and throw the picture on to a screen up to about 8 feet square.

As with any other piece of technical equipment, make absolutely certain that you know your way around the video player thoroughly, and rehearse its operation to the point of boredom.

Making your own video

Video-recording equipment is not really very expensive to buy. Unfortunately, the skills of television production are not so easily or cheaply acquired. Although the potential benefits of such equipment are clearly large, I would advise extreme caution until quite a lot of experience has been built up.

Obviously you can use the transmitting part of the equipment: it is the use of the recording part, the camera, that needs care. As long as it is simply pointed at places and objects and machines it will do no harm: the trouble starts when it is pointed at people. Every television producer knows the danger: the whole world has no sight to offer that is as spellbinding and satisfying as yourself talking out of a television screen.

Most people do it very badly (the natural ease of the television professional is a skilled technique that requires training and practice), but are still undeterred. A few learn to do it better, and become inordinately pleased with themselves. All of them talk about it with great modesty ('I don't really know if it comes off – Oh, do you think so?'), but they soon get hooked; they'd always thought they could do it better than those telly presenters if only they got the chance. Now they've got it.

You will never persuade the chairperson that there is even a second of boredom for the audience in a forty-five-minute medium close up of him or her saying what a fine future the company has if only everyone gets down to it and pulls together. Indeed if you work for such a person, it would be unwise to try. And so the danger of this equipment is that it will be used for interminable and counterproductive harangues by senior executives unleashing their egos in the name of internal communications.

Having said all that, I have to admit again that the potential of this equipment as a management aid is very great if it is properly used: but to discuss its proper use would involve the fundamentals of television production, theory and practice, which, like film-making techniques, are beyond the scope of this book. For presentations, the camera should be regarded just as a means of collecting moving visual material that cannot be as well presented in any other way (slide, OHP, model etc.).

If, despite all your efforts, you cannot keep people off the screen, try and persuade them to give some point to their use of the medium by doing what is impossible by letter, memo, circular or tape-recorder; such as sketching, handling a piece of machinery, showing new designs, pointing to particular details on a chart or diagram or balance sheet – any of these help to give a semblance of validity to what may otherwise appear to the recipient as naked and shameless self-glorification or indecent exposure of the ego.

Giant screen television and video

If you can afford it, this can use a satellite link-up to bring into a presentation live pictures of what is actually going on at that moment in factories, laboratories, stores, docks, refineries etc., all over the country, or indeed all round the world. However, it presents the complexities of a major television programme and needs professional help from the start.

More simply, it can be used just in the venue of the presentation to enlarge for a big audience a demonstration of something detailed happening on stage – the action of a small motor, a computer printing out – when the 'liveness' is too important to make a pre-recorded video the answer.

There is, however, a further possible use of the giant screen, and one which requires much more careful consideration: this is to point the camera at the speaker and throw their vastly enlarged picture on to the screen, a practice which is very common at big pop concerts. It sounds an excellent idea, but it carries with it a very grave danger.

The speaker–audience relationship

At the root of a good presentation lies the speaker–audience relationship (see Chapter 7): by turning the speaker into a television relay picture you can destroy that relationship and reduce the audience, who are kind of participants while the occasion is them-plus-the-speaker, into passive, uninvolved spectators. This is emphasised when speakers are moved to the side of the stage to give a clear view of the screen, and when the camera is placed between them and the audience for a full-face picture.

On the whole, therefore, it is a temptation which should be resisted. Only with an extremely large audience should it be considered at all, because then the advantages for the people at the back are much larger and the disadvantages smaller. If it is used in such a case, the camera should be well back in the auditorium on a long-focus lens, so that the presenters are in direct touch with most of the audience with the camera simply observing them. The screen can then be placed half-way back down the auditorium so that the front few hundred cannot see it and will consequently participate in the live presentation while the back ones, who would have been rather out of it otherwise, at least get a good view.

80

Visual aids – a means not an end
■ ■ ■

The final message of this chapter, however, must be the same as the first: visual aids are a means and not an end.

- Never include visuals for their own sake, and always be alert to the damage they can do.

- Never take great leaps into the dark with technical equipment – increase the complexity, if you must, very gradually.

- Always choose the least complicated of two kinds of visual aid if there is not much in it.

- Test the equipment and rehearse its operation – in the location if possible – until you have complete confidence in it.

And if you want a motto, the best one is 'keep it simple'.

Action checklist

1 Don't stand in front of visuals while you are using them.

2 Don't leave illustrations/charts/slides up after you have finished with them.

3 Don't turn away from the audience to draw/operate visuals more than you must.

4 Don't use a visual without referring to it.

5 Make sure all your visual aids are large enough and well enough lit to be visible to the whole audience.

6 Make sure you have spares of anything really important (OHPs, slides, working models etc.).

7 Be sufficiently comfortable with, and confident of, your visuals not to have to keep checking them when you're on stage.

8 Make sure you reveal visuals more frequently at low attention periods (well into a session, shortly after lunch etc.) to keep attention up.

9 Don't forget the value of physical objects as visuals.

10 Rehearse, rehearse and rehearse.

81

Thought-starters

1 *What are the visuals that you most remember having seen at presentations you have attended? What made them memorable?*

2 *Have you ever been irritated by the obtrusive use of visual aids? Why?*

3 *What is your attitude to using visual aids: do you regard them as an opportunity, a useful support, a necessary ingredient of presentations, a cross to bear?*

4 *What is the worst use or misuse of visual aids you've ever witnessed?*

5 *Do you have any deep-seated irrational fears or nightmares about how visual aids could let you down, even humiliate you? What can you do/check/rehearse to make sure your nightmare never becomes reality?*

6

Designing visual aids

The foundations of good slide and OHP design are common sense and clarity of intention. If your budget will run to a designer, meet a few and choose the one you seem to communicate with best. But if you cannot afford a designer, don't worry.

A sense of colour, line, composition, proportion and harmony, the gifts of visual invention and manual dexterity, knowledges of typefaces and colour psychology – these are fine if you can afford them, but you can produce an excellent presentation without them. I have seen enormously effective OHP/slide presentations put together unaided by groups in production engineering, computer applications and market development departments.

So if you know what you want the slides to do, go ahead and draw, paint or photograph them yourself. There are just three main areas where you have to be careful: planning the slides; the legibility of words; and the comprehensibility of pictures.

Planning
■ ■ ■

When planning a presentation the first question is not 'What slides do I need?': it is 'Do I need any slides at all?' The answer may well be 'No'. Let us first be clear about the disadvantages of visual aids:

- they take up a great deal of time and thought;
- they can divert attention away from what is to be said and on to how it is to be said;
- they diminish flexibility;
- they cost money;
- if they go wrong the result can vary from mild confusion to the ultimate in catastrophe and humiliation.

84

SO, WHY DO WE USE VISUALS AT ALL?

- A picture is worth a thousand words
- They can portray vividly and instantly things that are impossible to convey verbally
- They save time
- They create interest
- They bring variety
- They add impact
- They remain in the memory long after the words have left it

---

There is no question that a good presentation which employs visuals is enormously more effective than a good presentation without them. Usually the advantages outweigh the disadvantages, but the disadvantages are there.

If you do decide to use them, think about them from the very start, and make sure they are built into your presentation from the beginning. And, if you can manage it, space them out more widely at the start when the audience is fresh and alert, and bring them in with a greater frequency towards the end to keep interest alive.

There are four particular types of slide to concentrate on in the planning stage.

The unnecessary slide

The first question to ask about every visual is 'Can we manage just as well without it?' I sometimes suspect that up to one-third of all visuals used in presentations would be excluded by that question: I can hear some poor presenter being asked 'Do you want any visual aids?' and being shamed into saying yes for fear of appearing casual or lazy or amateur, and then dreaming up some slides or OHPs they don't want and which don't help.

The second question is 'Is this really a visual, or just a visible verbal?' If I could engrave a single sentence on every presenter's heart it would be this:

WORDS ARE NOT VISUALS

How many times have we sat at presentations and seen slide after slide portraying nothing except abstract nouns?

OBJECTIVES OPERATIONS	PREPARATION PLANNING PRODUCTIVITY PROGRESS	RECONNAISSANCE RECOGNITION REPORTING

85

These frequently go on and on in an endless and utterly unmemorable series. Words are what presenters are there for; they are provided with the complex and ingenious equipment of tongue, lips, teeth, pharynx, larynx and lungs in order to utter them. It is not possible to make a rule banning all words from visual aids, because they are sometimes necessary to help the audience identify pictures, and just occasionally an expert finds ways of using them effectively and dramatically; otherwise it would be an excellent rule.

Discipline yourself to ask 'What will this slide *show*?' and never 'What will this slide *say*?'

Those, then, are the two basic rules, which are very obvious when you state them baldly. A visual must be:

- necessary;
- visual.

The missing slide

A fault that is almost as common as the unnecessary slide (though far less obvious) is the missing slide. We must all have witnessed presentations in which the speaker confused or lost us completely by failing to use a picture to communicate a concept that was very hard to take in through the ears, but could have been easily absorbed through the eyes.

A reef knot or the film loading path of a projector are obvious instances, but there are many less obvious ones: comparisons of financial or statistical data are an outstanding example, where a judicious use of charts and graphs can instantly clarify and emphasise trends, proportions and relationships which are difficult to explain by words alone.

So, having planned your presentation and your essential slides together, it is still a good idea to go through it again looking out for the passages where a slide would help to clarify a complex idea or communicate an involved process.

The impact slide

A good discipline for anyone planning a presentation is to ask themselves what single point they most wish the audience to take away with them. A good way to put this is to ask yourself , 'As I sit down, what remark do I most want my 'target' listener to turn and make to the person next to them?' When you have identified that remark, you have identified the one slide you *must* include in your presentation and, what is more, the slide you must take most care over to ensure that it is striking enough to stay in the mind. It should ideally be the most visually memorable image of your whole presentation, and one you come back to more than once; it is frequently a good idea to leave it up on the screen as you finish.

The slide shown here is an example of the 'impact' slide for a presentation whose chief point is to make the audience realise that one bus can carry as many people as twelve cars, and the device of jamming the cars on top of each other gives the shock element which adds the impact.

The verbal slide

We have already looked at the fatuity of the abstract noun slide, but the verbal slide is worse than fatuous, it is destructive. For some reason it is particularly popular with presenters for using on OHP slides. The verbal slide is a slide consisting of whole statements, sometimes several of them numbered sequentially on a single slide. It is a killer.

It is a killer because, as we have already agreed, words are what presenters are there for, and what they are uniquely equipped to utter. But it is a killer for other reasons as well. In the first place, people all listen at the same speed – the speed of the speaker – but they all read at different speeds, so you immediately split your audience into groups who are mentally out of touch with you and each other.

In the second place, what are you to say while the words are on the screen? If you repeat the words verbatim, why have them on the slide? Are you trying to teach your audience to read? If you shut up completely, some will finish and be bored while others are still reading. If you say something different from the slide, you are making a basic communications howler, since no one can take in different verbal information simultaneously through eyes and ears. You cannot win.

In fact, most of the times I have seen this done (and that is plenty), the only conclusion I could reasonably make was that the speakers were projecting their lecture notes. I am all for lecture notes, but speakers should keep them on the table or the lectern or in their hand – they should never throw them up on the screen.

Readability

■ ■ ■

Too many words

We have already agreed not to use slides that consist only of words. But even pictorial slides can have too many words on them, and they often do. The words may be used to identify pictures or describe stages in a process, but whatever their intended task they will fail in it if there are too many of them. The audience are either deterred from reading them or fail to listen to the speaker because they are following the eye-words at the expense of the ear-words.

PUT
YOUR
MESSAGE
HERE

'Never put more words on a slide than you would put on a T-shirt' is a good motto. If you are still worried, there are two important points to bear in mind. First, a slide for use in a presentation does not have to be self-explanatory, and is often more effective if it cannot be properly understood until the speaker identifies and explains the picture. It is a support for presenters, not a substitute. The effect of slides is often increased if speakers bring them to life and breathe meaning into them as they take their audience through them. Secondly, some of the most intractable problems of slide design can be swiftly and easily resolved by giving the visual information progressively, over a sequence of slides, instead of trying to cram it all on to one.

89

Too small words

Another of the commonest word-faults is simply not making the words big enough. It sounds too obvious to be worth mentioning, but it is one of the easiest traps in the world to fall into.

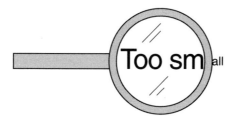
Too small

The trouble is that all the people responsible for the presentation know what the words are already, so they can read them easily. Moreover, they *want* the words to be big enough, because it is such a bore making the slide up all over again, so they kid themselves that the words are perfectly legible. And, on top of that, they often forget how far away from the screen some of the audience may be sitting.

The only safe course is to make the words (if you must have them) as big as possible, and to keep an active and lively suspicion that they are not big enough. And, once you have grounds for that suspicion, bring in a friend who does not know the slides, sit them in the back row, project the slides for them and make them call out all the words. If possible, do this in time to remake the slides if you need to: if not, note the words they have trouble with and make sure you say them out loud when giving the presentation.

Words at all angles

Words run in horizontal lines. It is the angle at which we are all taught to do our writing and reading, and any other angle presents us with the difficulty of the unfamiliar. The trouble is that pictures and charts do not all follow those lines, and it would be very boring if they did. This often tempts people to let lines on the picture dictate the angles of words. *This never works.*

The pie chart is, of course, the most common temptation: if the presenter writes words or numbers along the bicycle-spoke lines it becomes a custard pie chart. But it is still only one temptation among many. The only safe rule is *always* to write words horizontally, and to relate them to the object they identify by clear lines or arrows, perhaps aided by same-colour coding.

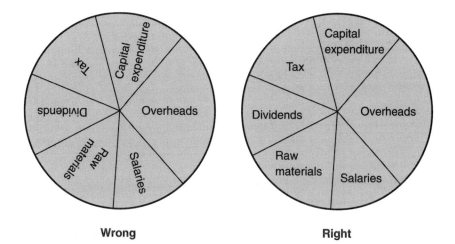

Wrong   Right

Colour camouflage

Of all the easy aids to successful OHP/slide design, colour is the one most frequently ignored by the non-professional, and in particular coloured backgrounds. It is not just that coloured backgrounds are infinitely more interesting than plain white ones: colours can also be used as codes. A review of sales revenue can use, say, red for Europe, blue for the USA and green for the rest of the world. This not only helps towards quick comprehension of bar charts and pie-charts, but it also enables the presenter to use coloured backgrounds for slides examining each separate market, so that the audiences are constantly reminded of which part of the world the speaker is talking about.

There is, however, one special trap for those who graduate from black-on-white to colour-on-colour, and that is camouflage. People do not often fall into this trap when they are simply using one colour on another colour: it is when they start to make colour differentiations between the foreground colours that they inadvertently put maroon on purple, and deep pink on light red. Even with white backgrounds you are not safe – a long-throw screen can make yellow-on-white virtually invisible.

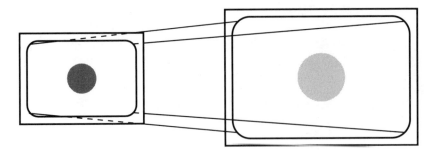

This problem gets more acute as you need more colours on the same slide. This is one of those points where you should ask yourself if a sequence of slides might not be better.

Just as an additional point: don't forget that once your audience gets above about fifteen or twenty, it starts to become likely that at least one or two of them will be colour blind to some extent. Red–green colour blindness is by far the most common form, so it is wise to avoid using these two colours in close proximity to each other.

Comprehensibility

■ ■ ■

I honestly believe I have never seen a slide that had too little visual or verbal information on it. By contrast, I have seen innumerable slides that tried to cram too much in. So when we are talking about comprehensibility, we are talking first and foremost about overcrowding.

There is no doubt at all what is the greatest single cause of the overcrowded slide: it is taking illustrations straight out of books, magazines or other printed sources. It is essential to realise that print is not speech. People can read to themselves at their own pace, and study a chart or a diagram in their own time: a complex flow diagram that takes three minutes to work through can be an excellent and invaluable adjunct to a book. It will be death on the screen.

But book illustrations, though certainly the chief culprit, are not the only ones. There is the permanent temptation to elaborate, augment and subdivide a visual illustration which every presenter has to learn to identify in themselves before they can conquer it. Often they are afraid that some expert in their audience will pick holes in their illustrations unless they are comprehensive and correct to the last irrelevant detail. They need have no such fears; it is the simplest thing in the world to say, 'Here in broad outline/in general terms/in a very simplified form ...' and they are covered.

So the general rule is reproduce print illustrations in a greatly simplified form (remembering you can often make up by adding colours much of what you lose by subtracting lines) and have the courage of your own clarification when producing your own original pictures. The words to engrave on your heart (and they are true of the whole presentation, not just the OHPs/slides) are:

93

KEEP IT SIMPLE

There are four particular areas where slides are most often overcomplicated.

Charts

Charts are a tremendous aid to communication. Pie charts are a marvellously simple way of showing what share of a total resource goes to which of the different applications. Bar charts and histograms convey relative sizes instantly. Graphs are unequalled for showing trends and variable relationships. The intelligent use of charts is often the solution to the hardest problems of communicating facts and figures.

But unfortunately charts, although they are inherently simple, are susceptible to endless complication by people who do not know when to stop. Extra lines and shadings get added, more and more facts and figures are put in, until the most beautiful and simple representation of a process, a proportion or a relationship becomes so unintelligible that it baffles or bores those whom it should interest and enlighten.

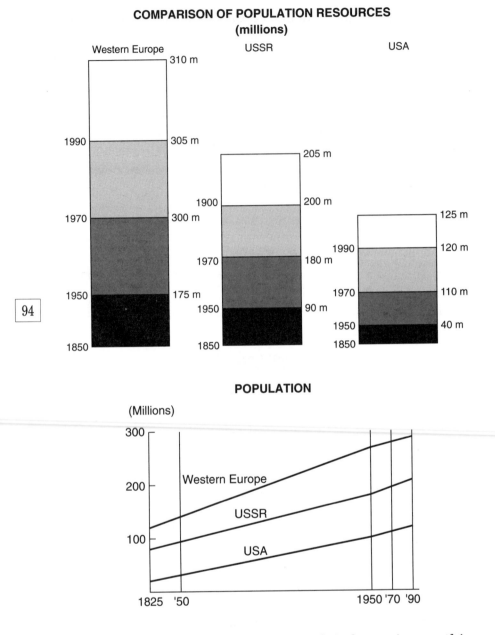

COMPARISON OF POPULATION RESOURCES
(millions)

POPULATION

94

As you can see, there is far too much information on this chart to take in at once. The rule with charts is to keep everything off them that you possibly can. You can add information verbally while you talk, and this often strengthens the chart as a communication device: and you can always –

usually with advantage – have a sequence of simple charts instead of a single complex one. But very often all you need to do, as with the chart above, is to remove the unnecessary information and find a way of representing the facts which *are* important more simply, see artwork p. 94.

Engineering drawings

Many slides are such a mass of boxes and arrows and feed-back control loops that you might as well put up a maze from a children's comic ('How can teddy get back to his home without crossing any lines?'). This distracts the audience from anything you have to say unless you work through it laboriously – and even then you will be too quick for some and too slow for others, or both.

The question that sorts the wheat from the chaff when considering an engineering drawing is not 'How does the machine/process/system work?', but 'What aspect of the machine/process/system must this slide illustrate?' The first question will land you with an incomprehensible jumble: the second will enable you to exclude all unnecessary details and concentrate on just those parts that matter for the point you are making.

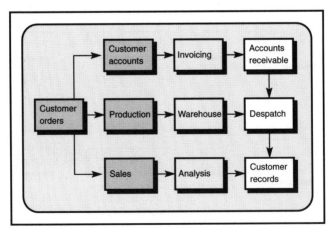

If you are photographing machinery (or anything else for that matter) the same rule applies. You can mask out on the photograph all those details that distract from what you want to show as follows:

- you can place coloured drapes or screens over inessentials before you photograph;

- you use close up to frame only what you want to show, and not a wide angle that includes its irrelevant environment;
- you use high key lighting to darken everything else;

- you use fast shutter speeds (and so wider aperture) to lessen the focal depth, and thus defocus and exclude background detail.

97

Interconnection

Procedures and processes can be a headache for the slide designer. It is often essential to show the paths taken by data through a computer, chemicals through a plant, documents through an office, or current through a circuit; but the resultant jumble of boxes, arrows and lines can mean ten minutes' hard concentration for the audience, while the speaker shuts up and watches them. If the presenter tries to take them through it, it's the usual problem – half of them get ahead and half of them don't keep up. So what do you do?

The answer, almost always, is to break it down first and then build it up gradually. It is not always easy, but a judicious use of colour codes can help, plus the device of 'masking down' (lowlighting) the sequences you have already been through as you bring up each new slide with the next part of the process, until finally you show it complete.

The two dangers to watch are:

- the temptation to take people through it too fast and in too few slides; and

■ failing to stop and remind them where you have got to and tell them where you are going next.

Tables of figures

On the whole, tables of figures are to be avoided in OHPs/slides. The information you want extracted from them is usually better displayed by graphic representation on a chart or diagram. It is not just that they can be confusing: they can also be too interesting, so that people start finding all sorts of fascinating information that is nothing to do with what you are using them to illustrate, and competes with what you are saying.

But if you have to use tables of figures there are two devices that can get you over this difficulty.

■ One is putting coloured rings around the figures you want to draw attention to, which works if there are only a few figures of significance on the chart.
■ The other is to mask down all the vertical columns or horizontal rows except the one (or ones) that matter for your purposes. And if you use this second device, you can always use the first with it to ring round certain figures within the highlighted row or column.

Close-up lens data

Close-up lens	Focus setting in feet	Lens to subject Distance in inches	Approximate field size for picture area in 2 × 2 inch slide	
			44 to 46 mm lens	50 mm lens
1+	Inf	39	21 × 30	18 × 26.5
	15	32.25	17.5 × 24.75	14.75 × 22
	3.5	20.5	10.5 × 15	9 × 13.25
2+	Inf	19.5	10.125 × 15	9 × 13.25
	15	17.75	9.25 × 13.625	8 × 12
	3.5	13.125	6.5 × 9.625	6.125 × 9
3+	Inf	13	6.75 × 10	6 × 8.875
	15	12.25	6.25 × 9.25	5.75 × 8.5
	3.5	9.75	4.875 × 7.25	4.5 × 6.375
3+ plus 3+	Inf	6.75	3.44 × 5.125	3 × 4.56
	15	6.5	3.31 × 4.875	2.95 × 4.375
	3.5	5.75	2.875 × 4.25	2.625 × 3.95

Action checklist

1 For every OHP/slide ask yourself 'Can we manage just as well without it?'

2 Remember that *words are not visuals*. Ask yourself 'What will this slide *show*?'

3 Never put more words on a slide than you would put on a T-shirt.

4 Make sure the words are set big enough to be read from the back of the audience.

5 Check you haven't missed out any illustrations that would help to explain complex ideas or processes.

6 Ask yourself what single point you most want the audience to take away with them, and then produce a slide to illustrate it, with impact.

7 Use colour to code your slides – but don't camouflage them.

8 Keep charts and drawings simple.

9 Use sequences of illustrations rather than one overcrowded one.

10 Use highlighting and masking out or masking down to clarify complicated photographs or diagrams.

Thought-starters

1 *What is the greatest number of words you have ever put on an OHP or slide? (Be honest!)*

2 *Have you ever been in an audience and been totally baffled by the complexity of some of the slides?*

3 *What would you do to try and avoid having to put an OHP/slide of a table of figures on the screen?*

4 *If you were giving a presentation and had to explain the layout of your nearest town or city, how would you go about it?*

5 *If you had to produce an impact slide to illustrate the most important benefit of your organisation's product or service, what would it be?*

7

The audience

There are three distinct types of audience, differentiated according to size and distinct in terms of how they respond to the presenter: a full audience of over one or two hundred, a presentation group of up to fifty or a hundred (with a somewhat grey area dividing the two), and a small audience of up to about a dozen. Since the response of each type of audience differs, it is obviously necessary for the presenters' approach to vary in order to achieve the reaction they want.

This chapter therefore looks at the different types of audience, and examines what style of presentation best suits each of them.

I once asked the French singer Juliette Greco about her attitude to a theatre full of people who had come to see her sing. She replied, 'I try and turn them all into one man – then I try to make him love me. If I can't, I go home.' I offer this not as advice to presenters – indeed it is not only impracticable but also probably most inappropriate – but as an insight into the nature of an audience from one of the world's experts in manipulating them.

The great paradox of audiences is that the larger they are, the more they become one person. Instead of becoming more diverse, they become more homogeneous. For the presenter there is an additional problem with increasing size: the larger the audience, the less they are reacting to what is being presented and the more to the person who is presenting it.

So far in this book I have tried to be logical and practical, and restrict myself to principles, practices and techniques. But I cannot properly explain what I believe to be the essential nature and function of the audience without becoming, if only briefly, theoretical and speculative. I do not think it matters very much if my theories and speculations are wrong, so long as they help to convey more clearly the deductions I have made after many observations and much thought.

Audiences and group behaviour
■ ■ ■

It is becoming more and more widely accepted that much of the behaviour of modern man is rooted in the prehistory of our species and of earlier ancestral species. Defence of territory and offspring, aggression, drives towards status and dominance, exploration, submissive behaviour – we exhibit all these characteristics today because they helped our species to survive in the past, and our predecessors who lacked them failed for that reason to become our ancestors.

Having for many years sat in audiences, addressed audiences, devised, produced and written television programmes for studio audiences, I am convinced that they are a modern expression of a primitive form of group behaviour which had survival value in the fairly distant past.

Just what that survival value was, we can only guess. But to me it appears that a large crowd of people packed together in one place achieves two important results that still cannot be so well achieved by any other means:

- the affirmation of unity and solidarity;
- the acclamation of leadership.

This is not true of small gatherings, but as they grow larger it becomes more and more true.

Large audiences

A really large audience is not, for most practical purposes, a place for detailed and reasoned argument. The more people there are, the smaller the proportion whose knowledge, experience, intelligence and interest are at the right level, and the harder it is for the argument to be comprehensible and relevant to any but a few.

When you get so many people together, you are not dealing with the intellectual differences of the individual but with the biological identity of the species. In a large audience we discover our group identity and we accord special prominence and respect to those who lead us to the discovery. It is not an occasion for new ideas.

103

THE PURPOSE OF A LARGE AUDIENCE

- Demonstrating which ideas the group accepts *as a group*
- Affirming group standards of conduct
- Publicly identifying threats to the group
- Proclaiming a shared resolve to march forward into the broad sunlit uplands
- Acclaiming those who will lead us to them

So, when is an audience not an audience?

In a television studio programme where laughter is required, most people feel uneasy until the numbers climb above two hundred. A burst of laughter is a good measure of whether a group of people have turned into an audience, but there is no absolute number for it; it depends on a number of factors.

Sixty people jammed into a tiny basement night club can be an audience, six hundred dotted around the Albert Hall can fail to become one.

I have dwelt on this at some length because it is of the most profound importance to presentations: if you have a full audience, you plan and execute differently in all sorts of ways.

104

WHAT DEFINES AN 'AUDIENCE'?

- Whether they are jammed together or scattered thinly around
- How well they knew each other before (jolly coach parties or individual people and couples arriving independently)
- Whether they have seen the performer before and how often
- Whether the auditorium is high and light, or low and dark
- The distance between the performer and the front row

Which kind of audience?
■ ■ ■

The great majority of presentations, in my experience, are not to full audiences, but presentations to full audiences are nearly always very important – even if the presenters do not realise it. But how do you tell if you have a presentation group or a full audience?

Before the arrival of the microphone it was easy. So long as you could reach everyone by talking in your normal voice, it was (and is) an ordinary group. But there comes a time when you have to raise your voice beyond the point where normal speech patterns can be retained. You have to shout, to declaim, to become an orator; if you don't, no one beyond the twelfth row will hear you.

This starts to affect what you can say. You can still cry: 'Shall we stand idly by when a crisis threatens all we believe in and strive for? Shall we let these unscrupulous villains ...' and so on.

It is much harder to shout to a thousand people: 'We will of course still use triplicated blue flimsy copies to indent for office equipment ...' All very sound stuff, but somehow not worth shouting about.

The trouble with the microphone is that it enables speakers to address five hundred people as if they were fifty, and the result is nearly always flat and disappointing. It is usually wise to try and reach the whole audience with the unaided voice, and look upon the microphone just as an insurance.

There is no point in going into any further detail about the point of division and demarcation between the two kinds of audience. There is obviously a broad overlap. What matters is to realise that there are two very different kinds of audience, one of fewer than fifty, and one of more than two hundred, and that there is an indeterminate area in the middle. For the purposes of this book I have had the small-group audience in mind, although virtually all I have said also holds true for a full audience. The purpose of this chapter is to emphasise that if the audience starts to creep up to and over a hundred or so, you have to start thinking very carefully.

What size of audience do you want?
■ ■ ■

The first question to ask yourself is whether you do in fact want a large audience. It all depends on what you are trying to achieve:

- Are you trying to persuade small groups of decision makers (*small*)?
- Do you want to influence a large body of decision accepters (*large*)?

- ■ Is your real purpose to affirm the unity and raise the morale of a large number of people (*large*)?
- ■ Is the aim to influence the attitudes, ideas and intentions of a few important people not under your authority (*small*)?

It is not a question of whether you are trying to persuade or not: all public speaking and indeed all writing is one form of persuasion or another. There is only one area of publication in which people proceed by remorselessly logical steps from unquestionable premises to unarguable conclusions, and it is called science. The beauty of science, and in particular of mathematics, is that you can convince without having to persuade. But in all other areas, persuasion is necessary: our question is simply about the means we use.

106 Where larger audiences are involved, you are most probably in full control of the time and venue, and deciding who to invite. So, if a large audience is the best means, assemble one: book a bigger hall and send invitations one or two further levels of management down the hierarchy. If a small group is the best means, and three hundred people want to come, hold five sessions during the day or on consecutive days (and remember that they are likely to improve as time goes on, so the last will probably be the most effective).

In the no man's land between fifty and two hundred you can have some influence by making the audience compact or scattered, by having house lights on or off, and most of all by the manner of the presenter (formal or relaxed, standing at lectern or sitting on table edge, etc.).

The speakers must be good enough
■ ■ ■

If you do want a large audience, you have another question. Are you a good enough speaker: if there are several speakers are they all good enough? It is not sufficient that they should be capable of addressing small groups – this is one whole grade higher in its demands, and you need speakers who have graduated or who you are sure have the ability to graduate.

Speakers who fail with a large audience, especially if they antagonise them, do themselves a great deal of harm. They pass into the folklore of the whole community as a bore, an idiot or a villain. If all the speakers fail the cause is lost.

This is equally true, of course, of small-group presentation, though the skills are more easily acquired. All the same, those who lack them should never be allowed to give any presentation of importance, however expert or senior they may be.

It may sound ridiculous to suggest that important decisions can hang on whether an audience likes someone or not – and certainly they will never admit it – but very often this is what turns the scale. I am talking about narrow decisions – not whether the airline needs new aircraft, but whose aircraft it should buy. The discussion will be about maintenance and range, consumption, passenger appeal and financial terms, and costs and price, and if one plane is clearly superior to its rivals that will be that.

107

But usually it is not so clear as that, and then the irrational starts to take over from the rational, feelings take over from arguments, emotion takes over from logic. People still talk about objective criteria – costs and consumption and maintenance – but they now use them not to reach rational conclusions but to reinforce irrational ones.

Up until the presentation the common ground will have been knowledge of the business and experience, and so on: the presentation often gives an extra ingredient for further decision making – a shared feeling about the kind of people who are trying to persuade them. People will have had private feelings before, but the presentation gives them shared ones. The more airline people who attend the stronger this will be (for better or worse). There will be a sort of consensus:

This becomes a much bigger factor than anyone will admit, and it is based very largely on the impression a few people made on a few other people in the course of a presentation.

I keep reading about decisions taken after totally unemotional logical discussion based exclusively on objective facts, but only in management books. Most narrow decisions, I am convinced, come down more often than anyone yet accepts to primitive tribal acclamation, to one individual or a small group of individuals winning the confidence and respect of another group. I do not even think it wrong that it should be so – very often this is in fact the most important remaining consideration. But we are taking a great risk if we are not aware of it when we are casting our presentations.

I doubt if an unsuitable group can effectively persuade their audience that they are suitable, but I have no doubt at all that a suitable one can, in the course of a presentation, convince them that they are unsuitable.

Pitfalls for good speakers
■ ■ ■

Apart from general incompetence of the kind the earlier chapters are directed at eradicating, there are two faults that most often beset otherwise good speakers. The first is unintentional arrogance.

Presentation speakers are usually in an odd position: they are raised up on a platform alone, whereas their superiors in status are shoved together in a group to listen to them. They have this position because of their authority on their own subject. The danger comes if they go outside this authority and begin to make assertions (even if correct) on subjects the audience believe they know more about. By using their special position for this purpose they are claiming superior status to them not in their own subject (which the audience concedes), but in the audience's (which is offensive and insulting).

A presenter of an aircraft must therefore be very careful to employ the formula of deference and submission when talking to the airline:

'The future of the airline business is for more and more planes on short routes and fewer but larger on trunk routes ...'

'It's not for me to tell you about the future of the airline business, but I understand from your own experts that you are expecting ...'

The second fault (not unconnected) is to wrestle when you should use judo. A presentation is very rarely the time to show people that their strongly held beliefs are erroneous. The most you can do is to accept their beliefs, but show that they have drawn wrong conclusions.

Intellectual judo is using the force of the other person's opinions and prejudices to win your argument. If you try and meet them head on you will not only lose, but risk antagonising them at the same time. Suppose you are proposing a corporate advertising campaign to a board that has already resisted the idea. It is better to join them than to try and beat them:

'I know some of you believe that corporate advertising is a waste of money, but in fact it is essential for any company that wants to move up from Division 2 to Division 1 ...'

'I know some of you believe that corporate advertising is a waste of money, and you are absolutely right. Most of it is just a very expensive way of massaging corporate egos. Having said that, there are certain specific corporate ojectives that are hard to achieve without it, and ...'

To reiterate the point made earlier, you have to get inside the listeners' minds at the planning stage and build your presentation on the foundation of their knowledge, prejudices, attitudes, experience and needs. If you spend all the time knocking away foundations, you won't build anything at all.

Questions from the audience
■ ■ ■

There is one small but important technical point: should there be questions from the audience? The following guidelines may be helpful.

Size of audience

The larger the audience, the more inhibiting it is to questioners. There is a feeling of 'Why me and not one of the 799 others?' and also 'My questions are only relevant to 10 per cent of this audience'. With very large audiences, up in the hundreds, questions are rarely a good idea.

Can it be damaging?

If you suspect that some, or any, of the audience are out to damage you, it is foolish to offer them the opportunity to do it publicly. It is perfectly reasonable to offer to answer questions individually and informally after the presentation.

Can it help?

Are the audience likely to feel they are being steam-rollered with sales talk? If there is a danger of this, they should be allowed a chance to say something before that feeling begins to grow. Are you worried that you may be slightly out of touch with their attitude or interests or level of comprehension? If so, their questions may give you valuable guidance.

When should questions be taken?

In principle, they should be taken after each separate section that may generate them. In instances where you think their questions may help you, the sooner the better. Also, questions are a useful texture variant (see Chapter 2).

The golden rule is that if you have any fears about questions, you should take them individually after the session and not during it. Their power to help a presentation is less than their power to damage it. Some questions are genuine requests for further information, but many are, in fact, some other response in disguise. These are a few of the principal types to look out for.

The concealed objection

It may indeed only be thinly concealed: 'Won't this mean weekend working?','Why is the price so high?', but can be dealt with according to the standard rules for objection handling:

- don't get defensive;
- make the objection specific;
- put it in perspective;
- give the compensating benefits.

The test question

This is designed to probe your knowledge and experience. 'What are the stress characteristics of this new alloy?' The golden rule is not to bluff or try to excuse your ignorance. If you don't know, promise to find out for the questioner – and keep the promise. In fact, it can be a useful excuse for coming back to them later.

The display question

Quite often a questioner's real motive is to show their colleagues how well informed they are. Nothing will make them happier than to have their expertise publicly commended, so don't be afraid to tell them how clever they are. 'Of course you're right. I didn't mention it because it's too technical for most people, and as you'll know it doesn't affect performance.'

The challenge question

You make an assertion which trespasses on the territory of one of the audience. It is best to retreat immediately and with deference, concede them full territorial rights in their area, and perhaps consult their wisdom. 'I'm sorry, of course I was only talking about the US market in general, not the US market for hot water bottles, which obviously you know much more about than I do. What in fact has been the sales trend over the past two years?'

The defensive question

Something you are proposing may mean a cut in staff, budget, status, authority, patronage or perks for one or more of the audience. 'What makes you think we can trust area managers to do their own purchasing of technical equipment?' may in fact mean 'Central purchasing is the part of my job I enjoy most, quite apart from all those bottles of Scotch around Christmas, and I'm damned if I'm going to let you take it away from me'. One way to deal with this is to question the questioner and get them talking more, and then if you have difficulty dealing with the point at the factual level try to throw it back to the rest of the group.

With any difficult question of any kind, your first reaction should be to quell any emotional response you may feel rising in your breast, and your second should be to explore the question, and ask the questioner to elaborate and refine it. You then have the various options suggested above.

OPTIONS FOR HANDLING DIFFICULT QUESTIONS

- Answer the question
- Admit ignorance and promise to find out the answer
- Defer it to deal with privately at greater length afterwards
- Refer it to an expert colleague if you have brought one
- Throw it back to the person who asked it
- Throw it back to another member of the audience
- Put it up for general discussion

One-person presentation
■ ■ ■

Finally, it is time to look at the very small presentation. So far in this chapter I have talked about two kinds of audience – the audience of less than fifty or a hundred, and the audience of more than two hundred. There is, of course, a third kind: the very small audience of about half a dozen usually invited (or visited) and addressed by a single presenter. Probably this is the most common kind of all, and it needs to be discussed separately.

The important point about a group of five or six is that it is not an audience at all. There is no question of individual identity merging into a single, anonymous unit. Just as it is clear that with six hundred other people in a hall you cannot all contribute your ideas, so with six people it is clear that you all can. Consequently, if one person does all the talking there is an implicit arrogance in their monopolising the meeting. This points to an important difference from larger presentations.

The difference is that with a larger audience you are the speaker and they are the listeners, asking their questions when you invite them, but with a small group you have to try and proceed by dialogue instead of monologue. Even if the group shows a disposition to remain a silent, passive audience, you must not let them.

At every stage you must invite them to participate:

The success of a presentation to a small group can be measured by the amount of time the presenter spends in listening to and answering questions.

The disadvantage of a small group – that you are spending your time getting through to only a handful of people – is balanced by the fact that those few people can be much more thoroughly convinced than a large audience. They go away with their objections met, their questions answered, and a sense of having thrashed the thing out. For this reason it tests presenters' knowledge of their subject more searchingly. They must really know their ground, and be very careful not to commit themselves to assertions they cannot support from their own knowledge and experience.

Conversely, a small group puts less strain on presentation aids and techniques. Slides will hardly be necessary, since half a dozen people can look at a drawing or a photograph without optical enlargement. If you do use them, it is not the end of the world if one or two come on upside down. The whole atmosphere is more relaxed, easy and informal, and the presenter should keep it so.

Nevertheless it is still a presentation, and all the principles stated earlier still apply, as follows.

- Presenters must plan what they have to say, and the order in which it has to be said.

- They must think themselves into their audience's minds – though the dialogue will be an enormous help to put them right where they went wrong.

- They need just as much care in selecting or designing the visuals they use.

- They need to vary the texture between words and pictures, between exposition and discussion.

- They need to check that all aids and equipment are present and in working order.

But the practicalities and techniques of one-person presentations need considerable modification.

115

The script

A formal prepared script, even in the most natural spoken English, is quite out of the question. The tone of the presentation is conversational dialogue, and must be spontaneous.

The shape

Spontaneous, however, does not mean unplanned. The presenter will have certain points to make in a certain order, and they must have these clearly in their head or written down in note form.

The texture

With such a small group it is not tolerable to hold the floor for more than a few minutes without letting them have their turn. The exposition must therefore be broken down into small chunks with discussion time after each – and the exposition itself must be liberally punctuated with check-up questions like 'Does that make sense?' 'Are you still with me?' etc.

Rehearsal

A formal rehearsal is, by definition, impossible. Nevertheless, a try-out with one or two colleagues as an audience is extremely valuable, especially if they can raise the sort of objections and questions you are likely to encounter.

Visuals

These need to be simple and flexible. Of course, any kind of visual aid can be used but slides, OHPs, video, magnet boards and so on are unnecessarily complex, and if not handled in a very relaxed yet competent manner they can bring an unwelcome note of contrivance and formality. The best aids for this sort of presentation are the following.

116

- *Whiteboard* It gives complete freedom to respond to any query that arises, and it can be handed over to any member of the audience who wants to make a visual point.

- *Flip chart* Same arguments as the whiteboard, and the additional advantage of not having to rub off and draw on traces of the last drawing.

- *Drawings and still photographs* These are easy to show to a small group, making whatever points you want according to the degree and level of their interest. You can also have a good supply of reserves which you do not plan to use but can produce if the conversation turns that way. A table lectern turned towards the group acts as a perfectly good stand if you want to leave one up for some time.

- *Solid objects* Anything you can pass round, or give to people to keep, is much easier with a small group and just as effective.

- *Working models* Anything real that people can actually see working is even better with a small group since they can all have a go at operating it if it isn't too difficult or dangerous.

■ *Videos* These are ideal for showing to small groups. They are often the only way of showing large equipment (aeroplanes, turbines, cranes, ships, machine tools) in operation.

But, in general, this sort of presentation hinges on the whiteboard or the flip chart, and drawings or photographs. The more you give the impression that you had got it all planned in advance, the less convincing it will be. For an example of this type of small presentation see Appendix II.

Summary of different skills for different audiences
■　■　■

It is dangerous to draw up rules about audiences, even to summarise a chapter: but there do seem to be certain distinctions between the skills you need to deal with large and small audiences.

LARGE AUDIENCES

■ **Maximum** performing skill as a speaker

■ **Maximum** slickness with visual aids and stage management

■ **Minimum** questions

If you succeed with a large audience, they will be impressed and may change their attitudes. If you succeed with a small group, they will be convinced and may change their minds.

SMALL AUDIENCES

- **Maximum** question and answer

- **Maximum** informality

- **Maximum** flexibility of order and content

- **Maximum** knowledge of your subject

- **Minimum** skill as a speaker and manipulator of visual aids

---

118

Action checklist

1 Decide what size of audience you want.

2 Make sure you are confident the speakers are good enough.

3 Don't allow yourself to sound arrogant when you are presenting.

4 Don't try to change your audience's beliefs.

5 Decide whether you will take questions during the presentation or privately afterwards.

6 If you are asked a difficult question, throw it back to the person who asked it, another member of the audience, or the whole group.

7 If you can't answer a question admit that you can't – and promise to find out the answer.

8 In one-person presentations, keep the atmosphere informal.

9 Keep the group involved and participating.

10 Use simpler, less formal visual aids when presenting to small groups.

Thought-starters

1 *What is the worst question you have ever been asked at a presentation? Did you handle it as well as you might?*

2 *If you are attending a presentation as one of a small group, what can the presenter do to make you feel more comfortable?*

3 *Do you feel any different when you are speaking to a large audience from when you are talking to a small group? How do you think this affects the way you come across?*

4 *When you are in a large audience, in what ways do your feelings towards the speaker differ from your feelings towards a presenter when you are in a small group?*

5 *What size of audience do you prefer speaking to, and why?*

119

.8
The last lap

By the time the day of the presentation arrives, almost all the factors that will determine its success or failure have already been decided. If conception, planning, preparation and rehearsal have been sensibly carried out, if proper thought has been given to words and pictures, and the relationship between them, then 90 per cent of the dangers have been removed. Presentations which look right at dress rehearsal very rarely go wrong on the day, however inexperienced the presenters.

Nevertheless, there remain certain areas which still need attention, and where a bad slip-up can be disconcerting. You can never foresee everything, but most of the pitfalls can be avoided if you know where they are most likely to be.

Venue
■ ■ ■

The decision on where to hold the presentation (assuming you were in control of it) will have been taken early in the planning stage, and some of the considerations have nothing to do with the mechanics of the presentation itself. Is it convenient for the audience to get to? Can we afford it? Is it posh enough? But if there is room for presentation factors to affect the choice, these are the main considerations.

- If you can possibly hold it on your own premises, do so. It significantly reduces the area of the unforeseeable and the uncontrollable.

- If you have to choose between a room that is slightly too small and one that is distinctly too large, choose the smaller. Obviously, if it is small to the point of discomfort it is ruled out. But a lot of empty space is depressing.

  Churchill insisted that the rebuilt House of Commons should not have as many seats as there were MPs. Much better to have them sitting in the aisles and standing at the back on the few great national occasions, than conduct most of the nation's business in a vast and almost empty cavern.

- Should the audience sit in a few rows on a wide frontage, or a lot of rows on a narrow frontage? I do not want to be dogmatic about this. I have a suspicion that an exact square may well be best; but, failing that, I would only use the wide and shallow shape with a fairly small audience that I wanted to treat extremely informally with a fair amount of questions and general conversation. If I wanted any sense of a show, or if the audience was over thirty or so, I would favour the narrow and deep alternative. Another important consideration when making this decision is sightlines, which are dealt with later in this chapter.

A square layout is probably the best

Narrow and deep gives more of a show

Wide and shallow is informal and good for audience participation

- Avoid too large a gap between the presenter and the front row. The closer everyone is the easier it is for them to hear and see, which is what presentation is all about.

- Obvious, but can be overlooked – check details of all technical facilities (lighting, power supply, which equipment the venue is providing, ventilation, fire regulations) far enough in advance to make any changes they may necessitate.

- Signpost corridors, if the building is at all labyrinthine, so that visitors can find their way to cloakrooms, buffets, bars etc. – and back.

- Sometimes the chosen venue is so booked up that a dress rehearsal on site cannot be arranged; for smaller presentations the venue may have been selected by the group it is being addressed to – perhaps potential clients – and access more than half an hour or so before the start of the actual presentation can be impossible. If the presentation is at all important or complex this is a very grave liability and serious thought should be given to holding it somewhere else. If you tell your potential clients that you do not feel you can do them justice with the venue as it stands, they will probably be happy to arrange better access or agree to hold the presentation in a place of your choice.

■ Dress rehearsal time should always be booked when the presentation time itself is being booked, usually for the previous day. The morning of an afternoon presentation is much less good – less time to get things done, and no chance to sleep on it all.

■ Have you got the room the wrong way round? Should the presentation area be the other end? This matters if, for instance, interesting distractions will be going on outside a window behind the presenter in full view of the audience, or if the presenter is right next to the only door so that all messengers, accidental intruders and late arrivals suddenly become part of the presentation as they open the door.

Don't arrange the room so that the speakers are silhouetted against a bright light, such as a window, preventing the audience from seeing their faces.

■ If you have not used the place for a presentation before, try and find someone who has, and ring them to find out if there are any snags or dodges to learn.

Dais layout

For a lavish and expensive production you may want to employ a professional designer. Do not look on such a person as an aesthetic mystic, and if they behave like one get rid of them. Of course you expect them to have some sort of visual taste and colour sense, but their chief talents are highly practical. They know a large number of the visual opportunities and problems that arise, and they know a wide range of techniques, materials and devices for meeting them. It is for you to make sure that they know what you are trying to do. The later you call them in the less value you will get – you'll have already taken a lot of their decisions yourself. The best time to do this is suggested in Chapter 3.

Don't tell them, 'We want an easel here, a green baize table here, and a flip chart here'; give them much more scope to help you. Tell them why you are doing the presentation, what you are hoping to achieve, and what the budget is, and ask them how they think you can best achieve it. The 'why' is very important: a lectern encrusted with rhinestones may be an attractive idea, but not if the presentation is to tell a government department you're so hard up that they must give you a research grant.

Lighting

There is a good deal of unnecessary mystique about lighting. Certainly some film and theatre lighting can be extremely complex, but for presentations it is only a question of logic based on common sense.

125

You are unlikely to need to convey a slow sunrise, a thunderstorm, or a torchlit procession in the street below: lighting for our purposes is simply to add clarity and focus attention, and logic says have lots of light on what you want the audience to look at, and little or none anywhere else. Be aware, however, that it is very hard on the eyes to look at someone or something starkly spotlit against total blackness for any great length of time, so it is often preferable to keep a low level of light on the rest of the stage to avoid this.

Spot lighting is therefore better than general lighting, and it usually helps if it is fairly powerful. The speaker needs the strongest light, and all visual aids (charts, diagrams, flip charts, models, whiteboards) need their light projected from the place that causes least shadow when they are in use. It is attractive to fade up each visual aid spot as needed and fade it out afterwards, but usually it is an unnecessary refinement.

Stage spotlights usually have flaps called barn doors which you can close to stop light spilling where you don't want it. The chief place where you don't want it is on the OHP/video/slide projection screen if you have one: though there is a story that an elderly lady member of a film society used to sit in the front row with a torch during foreign films, and shine it on the subtitles to help her to read them better.

Here is a handful of useful guidelines for lighting that is worth noting.

- The higher up you rig the spotlight, the more vertical the angle at which it hits the speaker or object it is trained on. This is a good thing, since it reduces the problem of inconvenient shadows, and gives speakers some measure of protection against blinding headaches caused by directing a light straight into their eyes. (There is a limit with this of course – direct vertical toplighting will simply make the speaker look like a particularly miserable Dracula.)

- Some visual aids flare badly under spotlights, and can be extremely irritating to look at. Sometimes careful angling of the light, or the object, will solve the problem, but the best solution is to spray the object with hairspray (assuming it isn't a priceless working model which will be ruined for ever), giving it a matt finish which reflects far less.

  Whiteboards are a bigger problem here, since you can't write on them if you have sprayed them. I think really the only solution here, if you can't change to a better angle, is to dispense with the whiteboard altogether if you can, and use a flip chart instead.

- Contact lenses are better than glasses for speakers, if you have the choice, since glasses can flare badly.

- Under strong lights, perspiration tends to make the face look very shiny. It is a good idea for speakers – men included – to powder their faces (and bald patches if necessary) to prevent this as it can be distracting. Any brand of compact powder, preferably translucent, will do.

- If the stage area beyond the speakers is in relative darkness, and if anyone is required to use a short flight of steps between the auditorium and the stage during the presentation, it is important to make sure there is at least some light on them so the speakers can see where the steps are; especially those speakers who are half blinded by having been standing in a spotlight for the last few minutes.

■ As a general rule, it is not a good idea to use strongly coloured lighting, except perhaps very briefly for dramatic effect. It can be tiring to the eyes, and it simply isn't as easy to see the person or object that is being lit.

■ It is imperative that any inexperienced presenter practises standing in their spotlight. They need to get the feel of when it is and isn't on them so that they don't wander out of it inadvertently during the presentation. In particular, they need to understand (and it is surprising how many professional actors have a problem with this) that if the light is hitting the stage at an angle, and creating a pool of light on the floor, the fact that their feet are in the pool on the floor *does not mean that their face is lit.*

127

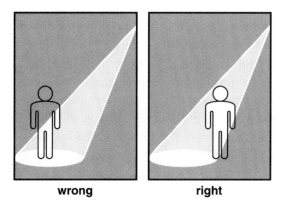

wrong　　　　**right**

■ If you have a presenter who has a habit of shuffling, fidgeting or transferring their weight from foot to foot while they speak, you will hopefully have trained them out of it before the big day. Failing that, however, don't direct a tight spotlight at someone if you can't trust them to stay in it. Better to have a wider pool of light with the speaker consistently in it.

■ If you want to try for lighting effects – fading up and down on appropriate places at appropriate points – remember that this requires a good knowledge of the script by the operator, and plenty of rehearsal. On the whole it is something to graduate to rather than start on.

Do not worry too much about lighting, however, for small presentations. General lighting will usually do well enough for numbers up to forty or fifty. Remember it can also help to focus attention on the whole presentation area. Sometimes the area can look rather lost in a large, high room, but if the bulbs over it are replaced with the brightest possible, with a solid shade that prohibits any uplighting, and the flexes lengthened until the light is only 9 feet above the ground, it becomes far more of a focus of attention. (Also, it casts an interesting shadow on the projection screen when slides are shown, and shatters when you accidentally hit it with your pointer – but that's what dress rehearsals are for.)

128

Decor

Again, this is not something to worry too much about. But sometimes the site has ugly pipes or unattractive walls, or distracting and irrelevant objects scattered around the place, and the judicious hanging of some reasonably coloured curtains, or some screening or cladding, can help the general appearance and usefully enclose the presentation area. Remember that coloured curtains often perk up wonderfully when you shine a bit of light on them.

And get someone else to take a look at the tables, chairs and so on that you are using on the stage – our eyes sometimes fail to see unsightly jumbles of modern teak, Victorian mahogany and reproduction Queen Anne in dark oak, that can easily be standardised if only someone thinks about it.

The auditorium itself does not often need much in the way of decor. But don't forget, especially if you're going to have coffee and tea breaks in it, that attractive and informative display panels around the edge can give people something to look at and also supply factual details that you do not want to weigh the presentation down with. If you are having breaks or a buffet lunch in a different room, you can have your display panels there. Producing display panels is a skill in itself which is outside the scope of this book. However, if you are planning anything at all ambitious it is well worth going into the subject in some detail before you design or commission your displays.

Stage setting

This problem only begins when you have a number of objects on the stage, and especially if there is a slide, OHP or video projection screen at the back. Then it can be quite a

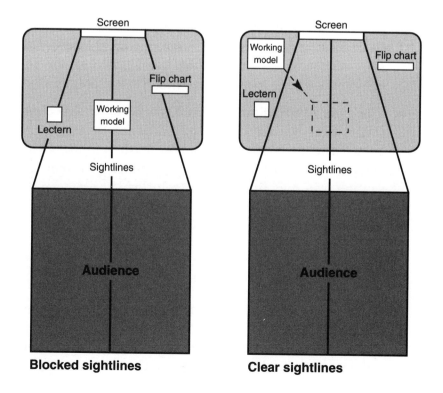

Blocked sightlines   **Clear sightlines**

headache. The problem is sightlines. You always find that, from one side of the audience or the other, something is obstructing the view of something else. Usually a flip chart is in front of the projection screen. Every time you move it you get another problem – different obstruction, light spill, masking by presenter or something else.

There's no general solution, it's just a three-dimensional jigsaw puzzle that you have to solve as best you can – but you must realise in time that you are setting it for yourself. There are one or two points worth making however.

- The only surefire way to establish where you have a sightline problem is to look at the stage from the auditorium. *You cannot check sightlines properly from the stage.* Get everyone who is available to wander around the auditorium during run-throughs and the dress rehearsal looking for trouble, as it were. Remember that every time you move anything on the stage (including people) you are potentially setting up another sightline problem which needs to be checked for; if there is going to be a lot of movement on stage during the presentation it's no good sorting out the sightlines for the opening positions and not checking them subsequently.

- The general principle, referred to earlier in this chapter, is that the narrower the audience frontage, the easier the problem is to solve. With a really wide frontage it can border on the impossible. With movable seating, you may find the best solution is to remove the edge seats on each row and use them to form an extra row or two at the back.

- The closer an object is to the audience, the more people's view it is likely to obstruct.

- If the stage is higher than the auditorium, the problem will be greater. If you are giving a large presentation in a venue where the auditorium is on a rake, the problem reduces considerably the higher up the seating you go.

■ One solution that sometimes works is to move objects into position just before you need them, and move them away afterwards. If you are only using the flip chart once, before the video projector, it doesn't matter if it blocks the screen as long as you move it to a back corner as soon as you have finished with it.

If you are going to do this, make sure you can do it smoothly and efficiently. You don't want to spend five minutes fumbling about trying to fold it up while everyone watches, only to give up in embarrassment and pick it up, dropping all the pens which were left on the ledge. As usual: rehearse.

■ If you are going to move an object, working model, flip chart or whatever into position during the presentation, there is a simple trick for getting it in the right place (to line up with the spotlight, the sightlines you checked in advance etc.). Set its position during rehearsals, and mark the floor discreetly with small pieces of coloured plastic tape at the points where the legs or corners go. If you are moving several pieces you can colour code them to avoid confusion. One word of caution: make sure that when you come to move the object into position there is sufficient light to be able to find the marks.

On the more positive side, it always helps if the stage has an appetising look for the audience when they arrive: not just in the orthodox design sense, but the look of a place where something interesting is about to happen. So don't always conceal all the things you don't want immediately; leave them in view – or leave them on the stage in an attractive box.

Dress
■ ■ ■

First impressions, as we are always being told, are vital. And a large part of the first impression we give is created by the way we look. There are certain key points to remember when dressing for a presentation.

- The most important rule is to dress appropriately. Research your audience. All organisations have their own dress codes; a large firm of management accountants will dress very differently from a small company of record producers. People like people who look like them, so adapt your outfit to tone in with your audience's style.

- Adapting to your audience's own style doesn't mean compromising on smartness. You will insult them if you turn up looking scruffy. Even if the audience look as if they have just been dragged backwards through a hedge, they will still expect you to look neat and smart.

- You can also encourage your audience with your image. For example, if you are a woman talking to a group of women returning to work after raising a family, they may not want to see someone who looks just like they do now. They want someone they can identify with, but who looks as if they've made it, so they feel they can make it too.

- If you are speaking to an audience of the opposite sex, don't go over the top trying to be like them. The woman who wears a feminine tailored suit to address a predominantly male audience will come across far better than one wearing a severe, masculine, pin-striped power-suit.

- Never let your appearance overpower your message. The audience has come to hear what you have to say, not to see what you are wearing. If you are presenting yourself as an authority on a subject, it will help if you appear responsible and authoritative in your dress, rather than showy or over-casual.

- Preparation is vital. Never leave it until the night before to decide what to wear. Decide some time in advance, and have it all ready, ironed and checked beforehand.

- Always carry a handkerchief with you – not a tissue.

- Women would be wise always to carry a spare pair of tights with them – and always wear a slip under a skirt if there's any chance you might need it, for instance if you are going to be talking with your back to a window or a strong light.

- Men should carry a spare tie, just in case anything gets spilt during lunch (the closer the match, the less likely anyone is to notice if you do have to swap).

There are certain things to make sure you avoid:

AVOID

- Extremes of fashion

- Revealing clothing

- Tight clothes that inhibit your movement or gestures

- Strong perfume or aftershave

- Jewellery that jangles when you move

- Old-fashioned styles

- New shoes or clothes that haven't been worn in

- Large patterns and bright colours over a large area.

133

And certain items will give you more of an air of authority than others:

TO AID AUTHORITY

- A jacket

- The darkest neutral colours that suit you, such as charcoal or navy

- Good-quality clothes

- A good pen

- Smart earrings for women (but not long and jangly)

- A good quality belt

- Some heels on women's shoes (not totally flat) – but not too high

---

134

There are more unwritten rules of dress for businessmen than women; you may get away with breaking them occasionally, but you need to know what they are first.

- If you are wearing a double-breasted jacket, always do it up when standing.
- Tie should be correct length – just to the waistband; not above or below it.
- Wear trouser waistband on navel and make sure trousers are the correct length:
  turn ups resting on shoe at front and blocked;
  non-turn ups slight break at front resting on shoe, slightly longer at back to where heel of shoe meets leather of shoe.
- Five-eighths of an inch of shirt cuff should show beneath jacket sleeve.
- Socks should be the same colour as shoes or trousers.
- Never wear pocket handkerchief *exactly* matching tie; better to pick up colour in tie or shirt.

There are fewer 'rules' for women, but there are one or two.

- Shoe colour should not be lighter than your hemline colour.

- Avoid fabrics with huge printed designs – they can overpower you and tire your audience's eyes. Wear strong or bright colours with detail nearer to your face to draw attention there.

Stage management
■ ■ ■

By this I don't just mean operations on the day; stage management is an aspect of the planning of the whole presentation, and it involves visualising the whole sequence.

Thinking through the sequence

135

Think the whole thing through in your mind pictorially and in detail – especially the junction points. Work out exactly what will happen, and what objects and actions will be needed at every point. How does x get off the stage? Where does he go? How does y get on? Where does she come from? Do they hand over the microphone or leave it on the lectern? If it is fixed to the lectern do you set it for your 6 foot 4 inch speaker or your 5 foot 1 inch speaker? If it is going to need adjusting, who adjusts it and when? Who has the pointer? Are the flip charts on from the start or do we set them? How does the slide projectionist know when to start the slide sequence?

There are hundreds of questions like this to be sorted out, resulting in a number of checks to be made before the presentation starts and certain actions to be taken while it is in progress. A checklist and notes in the script margin are the only answers and, if it is a big presentation, this needs to be one person's responsibility, though they may well be one of the understudies.

What if ...?

After all the questions based on the assumption that things go right, there is another sequence which starts 'What if ...?', based on the most possible of the most critical failures. What if the projector breaks down? What if the microphone doesn't work? What if the model doesn't arrive from the factory? Once the question is asked, the action to be taken is usually fairly clear, but it may involve preparations, so it must be asked in time.

Experienced stage managers usually have certain standard equipment always in their pocket: chalk, felt pens, drawing pins, PVC tape, penknife, screwdriver, razor blade, string, wire and nail file seem to be the most frequently employed – the nail file as thin steel lever, not for cosmetic purposes. A professional stage manager would have a small kit that also included:

- a range of basic tools such as: hammer and nails, adjust-able spanner, Stanley knife, screwdrivers (flathead and crosshead);
- gaffer tape (for taping down trailing leads that could be tripped over);
- fishing line (for tying things invisibly);
- hairspray (to stop shiny objects flaring under the lights);
- tape measure;
- blu-tac;
- anything the presenters might suddenly want like spare pens, highlighter pen, safety pins (for a hemline that suddenly tears), basic sewing kit;
- masking tape (to write on and use to label objects).

Microphones

If you cannot get by with the unaided human voice, sound coverage is rarely completely satisfactory. A microphone on the table is alright until the speaker goes over to the flip chart, then it loses them. If they take it with them it is a nuisance and volume varies depending on where they hold it. A lanyard microphone, hung round the neck like a pendant, solves that one, but you still have to worry about tripping over the cable or bringing the easel down with it. And it can be awkward to hand over if there is more than one presenter – it looks as if each speaker is investing their successor with the OBE. Many microphones also have a local on–off switch and, if the presenter forgets to turn it on (and it is surprisingly easy to forget), there is nothing the sound operator can do to help them.

To overcome the cable problem you can use a radio microphone (either hand-held or pinned to your jacket like the ones television presenters use) which has no cable, just a small, high-frequency transmitter carried in a belt pack. I used this once for a presentation to two thousand people in Leeds City Hall, and it turned out to be operating on the same frequency as one of the Leeds radiocab services. Taxi drivers' conversations blared across the hall at beautifully chosen points throughout the presentation. You can't win. To be fair, radio microphones usually work very well and are by far the best solution – you just can't count on them. If you have to hire or buy them yourself you will find they are also a good deal more expensive.

Even if the microphone is working perfectly, the speakers usually mistrust it, scratch it with their fingernails and say 'Can you hear me – testing – one-two-three ...' in jargon they have picked up from the sound technician. Do without microphones if you can, and get plenty of rehearsal in with them if you can't.

External interruptions

Some noises occur outside your building and your control. You will never foresee all the possible ones, but it helps if you are alert for them. Is the building on an air traffic route for certain wind conditions? Even your first visit may not tell you that – depending on wind direction. Are pneumatic drills going to be operating in the street? Does the children's playground outside the window make a presentation impossible during their break and lunch hour? Here, too, you may learn less painfully from other people's experience than from your own.

Internal interruptions

As with external interruptions you can draw on other people's experience, but it is also easier to be there on the relevant day of the week, and at the time of day, and see if any snags crop up.

Does a noisy potato-peeling machine start up in the kitchens immediately below at 11.30 a.m.? Is there a fire alarm and practice on the third Wednesday of alternate months? Do canteen workers play table tennis next door between 3.00 and 4.30 p.m.? When does the window cleaner get round to this side? Do cups and glasses clatter past to the directors' dining room from 12.00 to 12.30? Are people going to barge in thinking the room is empty if you don't put a sign on the door? Will four men be taking the carpet away for cleaning as the audience arrives? Again, you can never anticipate every possible interruption: the readiness is all.

Dress rehearsal
■ ■ ■

Try and take the dress rehearsal right through without any interruptions. If you pause you sometimes miss snags which continuity would have revealed. Make notes and go through them carefully at the end. It is sometimes a good idea to invite someone, who up until now has had nothing to do with the presentation, to look at it with a fresh eye. But this is no time to start criticising the presenters – there are two purposes in the dress rehearsal:

- to try out an already well-rehearsed presentation in its actual location, and see if any unexpected problems crop up because of the place, and its circumstances and facilities;
- to give those involved in the presentation experience and encouragement.

To have done the presentation in the actual territory is a source of confidence, but at this stage people want all the confidence they can get. It is a time for praise, congratulation and encouragement, and any visitors should know this in advance: serious worries should be voiced in private to the person in charge alone.

If correction has to be made at this stage it must be phrased most tactfully ('I wonder if it wouldn't be even more effective if ...') and followed up with unstinted praise ('That slide sequence goes marvellously now'). Professional actors sometimes need to have the fear of God put into them at this stage: with presenters I have found it is usually already there in abundance – it is hope of salvation they are short of.

The presentation
∎ ∎ ∎

139

Oddly enough, there isn't very much to say about the presentation itself. Or perhaps it isn't so odd: it is what the whole book has been about. The only special factor is first-night nerves, a kind of tension that communicates itself to everyone and can impair performance, and make people lose their heads and do stupid things.

Most people have some sort of butterflies-in-the-tummy feeling before doing a piece in public, and it is quite normal and natural. It is when the butterflies get out into the atmosphere that the trouble begins. If there is any danger of this, the temperature must be deliberately lowered by the producer of the presentation:

- they must adopt a deliberately casual approach, no sentences must start 'Whatever happens, for God's sake don't ...';
- they must appear to be taking the smoothness of the final presentation for granted;
- at the presentation itself there must be no urgent, whispered colloquy followed by someone hastening off at a thinly disguised run.

It also helps if a lot if those who will be doing the presenting have a chance to meet their audience informally before they start. A brief chat over a cup of coffee together can thaw out the atmosphere wonderfully. The presenters may even realise that their audience do presentations themselves from time to time, and feel much the same about it. Then if the most easy, natural and relaxed of the presenters does their piece first, you can begin to create the atmosphere you want – though the larger the audience the harder it is.

Making a success out of disaster

And in the right atmosphere, nothing can go really wrong. Even a disaster can be a plus. The damaging thing when the flip chart falls over is the presenter's shame, not the small interruption to the flow of their talk. If they see the joke, share it, and cap it, it can win the audience over to their side wonderfully.

I once saw a demonstrator show how a computer worked by sending tennis balls through a series of gates into a register selected by a programme which was another set of tennis balls. He explained how they would all go into register seven, forgot to load the programme, released them, and they shot straight into the zero. The audience rocked with laughter.

He clutched his head in delighted, theatrical distress, enjoying it with them. When the laughter subsided he said, 'That's exactly what I was saying. The computer is plain stupid. It does whatever you tell it, however crazy. A child of five would have heard what I was saying and put the data into the seven register. But the computer is a zombie – never helps you out. But if you programme it *correctly*, it never lets you down.' It was much better than getting it right first time, and in fact he kept the mistake in for ever afterwards. It is not the disaster which is the disaster – it is the presenter's wrong reaction to it.

What if it's going badly?

And suppose you can tell that the whole presentation is going badly – that there are impatient snuffles and shuffles coming out of the audience? It is difficult to cut and rearrange a complex presentation as it's running, but it may be possible. Speakers may speed up a bit, but there's not a lot they can do. Sometimes it's a good idea to put in a question session at the next junction, or even to ask the audience if there are things they are more interested in than what the programme contains, and dissolve the presentation into a seminar. After all, it is the audience you are doing it for: if they are disliking it, there is not much point in gritting your teeth and going right on, and to hell with them.

Afterwards
■ ■ ■

141

So, it's all over. It was a great success, everyone did splendidly, and a mood of euphoria settles on everyone. This is no time for cool appraisals but warm congratulations. ('Oh, do you really think it went all right?' which is English for 'Don't stop praising me, I'm enjoying it'.) But, if it was really a success, the chances are that you will be called on to give other presentations, and this one will have generated a lot of raw experience which can be worked into a body of knowledge.

A week or more later is the time to talk over the lessons to be learned, if possible with all those who took an important part and someone who was in the audience for the first time, and to make notes. This is the only real way to learn about visual presentation. A book is like a map – it gives a picture of the terrain, it shows the good and bad routes, the cul de sacs and short cuts, the dangerous cliffs and the quagmires. But it does not actually get you anywhere – you still have to make the journey yourself:

> 'I hear and forget, I see and remember,
> I do and understand.'

Action checklist

1 Check all the technical details thoroughly – power supply, equipment etc.

2 Make sure you are using the room the best way round.

3 Contact other people who have used the same venue and draw on their experience.

4 Keep the lighting simple, and rehearse with it thoroughly.

5 Make sure, from the auditorium, that no sightlines are blocked at any stage of the presentation.

6 Dress appropriately to suit the audience.

7 Think through the whole sequence of events from a practical point of view – where are the props and microphones, who moves where, and when?

8 Ask yourself 'What if ...?' to prepare for the worst possible breakdowns and failures.

9 Identify as many potential interruptions as you can – internal and external.

10 Once you reach the dress rehearsal, all comments should be encouraging, supportive and inspire confidence.

Thought-starters

1 *What did you wear at the last presentation you gave? Why did you choose that outfit?*

2 *What's the least helpful thing a presentation producer or boss has said to you just before you've gone 'on stage'?*

3 *How many potential interruptions can you foresee if you had to give a presentation in the room (or train, plane, garden etc.) you are in now?*

4 *If you have attended a presentation post mortem before, how helpful was it? Could you have improved on it?*

5 *How many rules for giving presentations have you learnt either by getting it wrong once, or by watching other people get it wrong?*

._. .9

Commissioning a video

Any important presentation is liable to need a video sequence or sequences specially shot for inclusion; furthermore a video itself is a presentation of a particularly durable, controllable and usually expensive kind.

Video making is of course a task for specialists and beyond the scope of this book, but anyone concerned with presentations may at some time have to commission a video and, unless it is done right (and it is easy to do wrong), it is a very efficient way of wasting a lot of time, effort and money.

Equally, someone who needs a video may be deterred by simply not knowing how to set about it. So here are some basic guidelines which, while they cannot ensure a good video, will enable anyone who follows them to avoid nearly all the obstacles that stop good videos happening.

Do you really want a video
■ ■ ■

It is easy to say 'We need a video' and the idea is an intoxi-cating one. The very idea awakes echoes of Hollywood movies – Cecil B. De Mille and Elizabeth Taylor and swim-ming pools in Beverly Hills. But perhaps your purposes would be better served by a book, a live presentation sequence, or a sequence of stills printed on to video with an added commen-tary, so that you show it through a projector but never employ a video camera. Video has several disadvantages.

- It is expensive, and often unnecessarily so since the details are usually outside the comprehension of the sponsor.

- It is a pig in a poke – you can't see it before you buy it, and when you can see it it's too late to discover it is not what you wanted.

- It prohibits participation – you can't ask a video a question.

- It is inflexible – you can't adapt it for special audiences as you can adapt a live presentation.

- It can become outdated – new buildings, equipment, products, policies, names and faces can make it obso-lete before full value has been extracted from it.

- It takes a longish time from conception to execution, and can be at the mercy of second, third and fourth thoughts.

- Chairpersons, presidents, chief executives and board members who would never dream of dropping in on a presentation will often order a screening of a video. Fear of this can create jitters among subordinates resulting in the removal of anything arresting or origi-nal from the film.

The advantages are more obvious: it is the most complete and powerful form of communication, it commands total attention in a way the printed word cannot, it can bring before people's eyes pictures of things that move, collected from all over the world, through telescopes and microscopes and stroboscopes, in fast or slow motion; you can constantly adjust pictures and words until you have them right, then you can distribute copies all over the world knowing that it will be shown in the form you intended. Inflexibility is also reliability. Nevertheless, it is a mistake to assume the need for a video before properly analysing the objectives and alternative means of achieving them.

Who should make it?
■ ■ ■

The video is going to succeed or fail because of two people: one is you, the sponsor, and the other is the video maker. So, how do you find a video maker?

Look at some videos

It is a great risk to get a video made by someone whose videos you have not seen. If you have seen a video that you thought was good, and it was also the kind of video you want, approach the maker of it. But the kind of video is important: a good video of engineering processes is no guide to ability in putting over theoretical concepts. If someone is recommended, look at one or two of their videos before you meet them.

Videos are made by people, not companies

You are looking for the person who made the video you liked, not the company. Of course the person may still be with them, but in this sort of business people move round quite a lot. Be very careful of putting yourself in the hands of a video production company unless you have seen a range of good videos by them which a variety of different people have written and directed.

Who makes a video?

How do you know who is the person who actually made the video? Are they called producer or director? There is no answer to the second question: the answer to the first can be obtained by a call to the people the video was made for. They are always clear about who was answerable to them for the success or failure of the video, and whether they were called producer or director or production supervisor doesn't matter a damn.

What should you look for in a video?

This is almost impossible to answer without descending into laborious detail or retreating into mystical words like 'flair' and 'impact' which are almost meaningless. The best guide is a purely personal one – your feelings about the video as it ends; if it leaves you with the feelings and attitudes which it set out to arouse, it has succeeded.

JUDGING A GOOD VIDEO

- It set out to make you believe that half the accidents in engineering shops could be avoided by a single half-hour induction course for all recruits, and you reached the end of the video convinced that this was so: fine, that is the main point of it all.

- You never got bored: the video always kept you wanting to know what was coming next.

- You could take it all in: nothing was too padded or too compressed or too confusing, either visually or verbally, and there were no stretches of commentary that were too long to listen to.

- It was properly thought out: it had the right facts and the right pictures in the right places to make its points.

- It was all relevant: there were no sequences which added nothing and could have been left out.

If those five conditions are met, you are on to a good thing. Dramatic climax, side-splitting humour, breathtaking pictures, unbearable suspense – all these are splendid if you can employ them and afford them, but I'd settle for the more mundane standards of efficiency.

What should you look for in a producer?

This is almost harder than the last question. Certainly they should have an open mind about what sort of video it should be, until they have a good understanding of what you want to achieve. It is a danger sign if they seem more concerned with the video they are making than with the objectives you want to achieve. It's also a danger sign if they don't ask many questions or admit their own ignorance about your subject, and if they give the impression they can achieve whatever you want: they ought to be referring your aspirations to the realities of budget and cameras, and microphones and audiences.

147

It's another danger sign if they seem concerned only with satisfying you, rather than with satisfying the audience you want to show the video to. And, although in principle I dislike this kind of advice, it is important that you should feel you can get on with them: the sponsor–producer relationship can be subjected to quite severe pressures, and flaws can be ruthlessly exposed.

If you cannot find anyone whom you really feel in your heart you want to make this video with, you should really think very seriously about whether to go on with it. Much better abandon it now than go ahead with the best of a bad bunch.

The sponsor and the producer
■ ■ ■

All right, you've chosen your producer. Their videos have impressed you, the sponsors speak well of them. They're interested, they ask intelligent questions, they seem to understand something of your sort of business, you trust them and you like them. You are already half-way home, and it doesn't matter if it took a great deal of time and trouble to find them: the choice of the producer is by far the most significant single determinant of the success of the video. However, you are both different kinds of animal and a chasm still divides you. You must set about building a bridge.

This chasm is a communication chasm. You understand your firm's business backwards –its history, its power structure, its internal tensions, its external successes and failures, its pride and its prejudices. Producers know virtually nothing of this. They do, however, know about editing suites and stop-frame animation, and cranes, dollies and lip synching, and when they talk about paintboxes it never occurs to them that you think they mean a small tin of dry watercolours that you mix with water.

They command a wide range of tools and techniques for achieving your objectives – but they do not yet know what your objectives are, and they will not understand if you tell them since they have not yet the background knowledge to give them a frame of reference.

148

Exchanging information

This brings us to the crux of the relationship, and many videos founder because it is not properly understood. Think for a moment in terms of an architect designing you a house. You do not draw them the house you want – if you're that expert, all you need is a building contractor. You tell them how much you can afford and how you want to use the house, and the priorities. It's their job to offer you suggestions and alternatives.

Is a south aspect more important than a large garden? Do you want to eat in the kitchen? Is good sound insulation more important than good heat insulation? Had you thought of tiling the kitchen window-sills? Do you realise that by moving these two radiators nearer the centre of the house you could manage with a smaller boiler? They are constantly forcing you to think harder about what you really want, and getting more and more insight into your objectives.

In this respect video producers are very like architects. If you tell them the pictures you want and the commentary you want, you are usurping their role and wasting their talents. They can almost certainly do better for you than that. To bridge the chasm, you must help them to the fullest possible understanding of the end result you are trying to achieve, and they must offer you suggestions and alternatives.

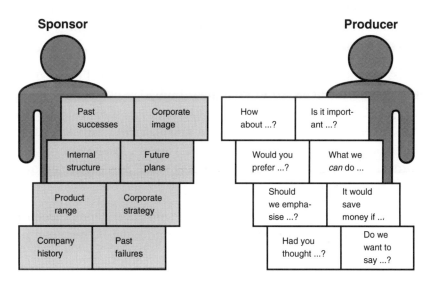

149

They will begin to see what you are after, and you will begin to see the implications of various decisions. If the film is to be highly technical, it cannot also be shown to schools for recruitment. If you want to film in the African factory you cannot also afford the cartoon sequence. If you have lots of people talking on camera, there will be problems in the foreign language versions. And so on. This is quite a long dialogue, and you must not try to rush it: you should also encourage the producer to talk to other members of the organisation, if only to sort out what is generally accepted and what is just your point of view.

The producer's authority

One other point must be established from the start, and that is the producer's authority. It must be made clear to them, and more particularly to all your subordinates, that they take orders from you and you alone. There is a special reason why this is important: everybody who holds any authority under you is likely to feel responsible for what is in the video if they are involved in it or are asked questions, and to dread that the moment the managing director sees it they will be fired. This induces a paralysing caution, a determination to agree to nothing except the most innocuous and trite words and pictures. If they know it is not their responsibility, the terror is removed.

This, of course, is all very well if you are making the video on your own authority, from your own budget, and for your own purpose. If your boss is doing this, but has delegated it to you, make him or her read this chapter and think again. There remains the possibility that you are responsible to a committee. This can work perfectly well, provided certain conditions are met.

- The committee must be small – not more than three or four, plus you and the producer – and must be representative. You don't want the most pliable or the most progressive, you want sensible, middle-of-the-road people.

- The committee must be taken fully into the producer's confidence, and really talk things through at the earliest stages, before shooting. This not only helps the producer – it also implicates the committee in the video if they have agreed the salient points.

- The committee must give full editorial authority to the producer. They retain, of course, the right to be consulted, the right of veto on grounds of fact or policy, and the right to scrap the whole thing. But if they have editorial authority they are answerable to their colleagues for everything that is included, everything that is omitted, and the way everything is done. Such a heavy burden may break their nerve. Much easier if they can say 'Yes, we didn't like that bit either, but we only had the power to advise or veto, we

couldn't improve anything'. Wise producers will ask
for that editorial freedom before they go ahead, and
have no reason or incentive to abuse it.

Agreeing objectives

The purpose of the dialogue between the sponsor (with or
without the advisory committee) and the producer is to reach
agreement on an objective which both of them fully understand. A useful means to this end is to define your key
audience – a new graduate thinking about a career, the production manager of an engineering firm, the chief executive
of a medium-sized company – and then to formulate the sentence you want to be in your audience's mind when the
projector stops and the lights go up.

This agreement about objectives demands great honesty
from the sponsor:

151

- the producer must be told about departmental rivalries
  and jealousies which will make certain desirable ingredients difficult and dangerous;

- they must be told where the firm has unsuccessful
  products or a bad reputation;

- they must be told of subsidiary, even if ignoble, motives
  behind the commissioning of the video ('Marketing did
  a good video last year which made quite a star out of
  the marketing director, and the production director
  really agreed to this out of personal jealousy, so it will
  be difficult to leave him out completely').

Part of the difficulty in getting the dialogue under way is
that dialogue is conducted with words but videos are made
with pictures. Inevitably when you decided on a video you
had certain pictures in mind, and you may believe you have
conveyed them to the producer: you probably haven't. So do
not be ashamed to draw lots of very bad rough sketches in
screen-shaped boxes to show them what you mean, but make

it clear that your purpose is not to make them take those pictures, only to convey to them what you are thinking of.

Practical decisions
■ ■ ■

How long should it run?

If you run the video longer than about twenty-five or thirty minutes, you are setting yourself a lot of problems. The chief one is holding the audience's attention – the video needs to be that much more entertaining if it is to run longer than half an hour. It is also harder to get people to give up the best part of an hour of their time rather than just twenty minutes or so, and if the video is part of a presentation it is likely to take it over if it runs too long. If it is ever to be used in discussions or seminars a shorter video gives time for introduction and discussion within a forty-minute period.

152

Setting about it
■ ■ ■

Before you commit yourself to a producer you should establish two stages at which you can pull out – after the treatment, and after the shooting script.

The treatment

All too often this is just a sales document disguised as an outline of the video: 'The video will show in compelling and vivid detail ...dramatically contrasting ... leading the audience into the throbbing heart of ... rising to a climax ...' etc. All you are looking for is a simple outline of what will be shown and said in the video, and you will judge from that whether the producer understands what you are trying to achieve.

The treatment should not be more than a dozen pages or so, but the cost could easily be a four-figure sum, since if it is to be done properly there is a fair amount of preliminary research and discussion to be carried out first. My own view is that a good treatment is so much more important than anything else that it is often worth paying double in order that the producer can afford to spend longer getting to understand your objectives before committing anything to paper. Once they have decided on a treatment it is hard for them to put it all back in the melting pot.

The shooting script

Unlike the treatment, this is an operational document. It is usually divided into two columns, one saying what the audience will see, and the other saying what they will hear. It is the nearest you will get to seeing the video you are commissioning before you commit yourself to paying for it, but it is all too easy for a layperson to misunderstand it.

153

To start with, it is almost impossible to see how music, sound effects, camera work and editing will combine to produce an effect on the audience. In addition, the picture column is full of technical jargon – mix, track, pan, dissolve, m.c.u., w/a, s/i and the rest of it – which diverts concentration on to the commentary/dialogue column. This, however, is most misleading when just read on its own and, in the case of commentary, can be changed even after the shooting is over: the shooting script only commits you to pictures and synchronous sound.

So do not hope to judge from the shooting script whether it will be a good video. Look for:

- errors of fact;
- pictures wrongly included;
- pictures whose significance seems to be misunderstood;
- pictures omitted which you think should be included.

When reading and discussing the shooting script – and this applies at all later stages as well – there is one vital point to bear in mind. If the producer is any good, they are not making this video to show to you or your company: they are making it for the audiences you are going to show it to. A paean of unqualified praise lasting thirty minutes may delight all the members of your company, but it will leave everyone else cold.

The producer, as an outsider, is likely to be a better judge than you of how to interest your audience. The company may judge the video by whether it says and shows all the things they want said and shown, but its success (assuming it is not being made exclusively for internal use) will depend on how many people outside the company see it. The more interesting and enjoyable it is for them, the more attention they will pay to it and the more they will recommend it – and also the more respect they will have for people capable of holding their interest.

It is hard to say how much you should pay for a shooting script – it may involve a lot of time by the producer, director and writer, even including overseas travel. It is probably best to agree a rejection fee before you commission it – a sum to be paid if you decide not to go ahead after its completion. You must expect it to be three or four times as much as the cost of the treatment. If you do go ahead, it becomes part of the total cost of the video.

Budget

■ ■ ■

Once the shooting script is complete, a reasonably accurate budget becomes possible. Some production companies may try and present it to you as a single, global figure, but you should make it clear from the start that you will want a detailed breakdown before going ahead. This is not so much because it is harder to fiddle a detailed budget as to give you an opportunity to realise the cost implications of various production decisions.

You may have asked for shots in factories in five different cities: the travel and subsistence figure will prompt an inquiry into how much cheaper it would be to take them all in one city. The special equipment bill may reveal to you that a casual remark of yours about taking a wide shot of the milling shop when it's empty has been translated as a vast lorry-load of lights being driven down from London, with weekend overtime rates for everyone.

An example of the sort of budget breakdown you will need is included below, but generally speaking the expensive variables which can be reduced by modifying the shooting script are as follows.

- Animation, especially cartoon animation.

- The lighting of large areas for a single shot (expensive not only for the lights but also for the time it takes to set up).

- Using a full sound crew when a silent camera would do almost as well.

- Travel, especially overseas, and subsistence. Quite apart from the direct expense, crew time is spent travelling instead of shooting. Think about including still photographs of remote locations you would like to include, or – for overseas shooting – getting a local camera operator to take some shots and post them back.

- Overnight and weekend shooting when overtime has to be paid.

- Outside location shooting when special weather conditions are essential, e.g. where you may have to spend days just waiting for bright sunlight, heavy rain, snow etc. If almost any weather conditions will do, outside location shooting – since it needs no lights – is quick and cheap.

155

There is one other important budget consideration, and that is the payment of the producer. If the video is being made by a production company which has its own cameras and editing machines, their profit will be a percentage of the total cost. This, of course, gives them an incentive to make the video as expensive as possible. If this worries you, it may be possible to engage an independent producer and agree their fee irrespective of the budget: they will then have an incentive to work with you to keep all the other costs as low as possible.

SPECIMEN VIDEO BUDGET BREAKDOWN

£

Studio, crew and equipment time

...days	studio hire at.....per day	——
...days	filming at.....per day	——
...days	sound recording at.....per day	——
...days	camera hire	——
...days	camera accessories hire	——
...days	lighting hire...	——
rolls	videotape at.....per day	

Post production
Off line editing ——
On-line editing and digital effects ——
Tape and transfer costs ——
Dubbing ——

Travel and subsistence

...days	car mileage at.....per day	——
...days	extra car hire at.....per day	——
...days	subsistence at.....per day	——

Train fares (details) ——
Boat fares (details) ——
Air fares (details) ——
Freight charges (details) ——
Entertainment, permissions, facilities

Special effects
Titles and graphic work ——
Computer animation ——
Rostrum work ——
Still photography ——

Artistes, rights etc.
Music rights ——
Copyright ——
Stills copyright ——
Film copyright (library film) ——
Actors/narrators ——
Musicians ——

Production
Scenery, props, make-up ——
Producer ——
Director ——
Writer ——
Designer ——
Administration and overheads ——

Add 10% contingency ——

Total ——

It must also be understood that once the budget is agreed, it is not just a general guide for you: it is a firm undertaking by the producer or the production company that the video will be delivered for that sum.

The point of no return
■ ■ ■

Once you have agreed the shooting script and the budget, and given the go-ahead, you have passed the point of no return. There is very little you can do to affect the video until shooting is completed. It is usually wise, however, to fix the following dates by agreement with the producer and check periodically that they are not slipping – or not too badly:

- the date when shooting will start;
- the date when shooting will end;
- the date when you will be able to see a roughcut.

157

The roughcut is the next point at which you get involved in the video. It is a rough assembly of the pictures in sequence, but probably a good 50 per cent longer than the final version, and it is unlikely to have any commentary. As with the shooting script it is hard for the layperson to foresee or deduce the final effect of the completed video by seeing the roughcut.

At this stage the producer and their team need confidence and encouragement, and unless you are gravely worried you should try and give them some. If you can see that it is all hopeless, that nothing you wanted is there, you can cut your losses by calling the whole thing off straight away, but you are unlikely to save more than 20 per cent of the budget from the wreck.

But, if the roughcut includes most of the pictures you wanted, you will serve your own purposes best by distributing general praise and admiration. You can then get down to details, and the details that concern you are not those that make it a good or bad video: they are those on which you are specially qualified to speak:

- factual and pictorial accuracy;
- order of sequences;
- company policy;
- the intention and objectives of the video as a whole.

Be particularly careful to mention what you think it is important to keep in, because there is still quite a lot of cutting to do. When you leave, fix a date for seeing the final assembly with commentary.

You may be sent a copy of the commentary to read, though experience has made many producers reluctant to do this. If you do receive a copy, for heaven's sake do not start rewriting it: it is intimately related to pictures, music and sound effects in ways you cannot possibly know about. Make your comments on a separate sheet of paper, and try and restrict them to what is wrong with the commentary rather than your recommended version: 'This does not give the most important fact ... this emphasises the wrong aspect ... this gives the impression that we only ... this figure is the national, not the world, production ...' etc.

Treat it like a fitting at the tailor's or dressmaker's: you tell them where the outfit feels too tight or too loose or hangs badly, but you would never dream of getting out a piece of chalk and drawing marks on the cloth. A commentary is tailor-made to the video in the same way, and you have just as little qualification to carry out the alterations yourself.

Resist the urge to alter

The trouble with commentary is that it looks so easy to alter, and consequently a great many videos which might otherwise have survived and flourished are killed by commentary. The lethal element in commentary is the overdose. A good video will leave many gaps in commentary, and the story will be taken forward by pictures with sound effects or music or actuality sound. Commentary alterations usually mean additions, and the vital gaps start to disappear, with the self-defeating result that the audience simply cannot take any of it in.

In particular, try to restrain yourself from asking for additional words for company rather than audience reasons: 'The Birmingham factory will be unhappy if we don't mention ... the research people would like it if we said that they ...' and so on. There is a limit to what the audience can absorb as video commentary, and the writer is trying to keep it simple and sparing. Of course, you must correct errors of fact, emphasis, omission and policy, but it is better to think of the overall duration of each paragraph as immutable.

Once the commentary is agreed, the video is complete as far as you are concerned. There is nothing to do but fix a date for the delivery of the final copy, invite the guests to the première, and make sure the drinks are served before the viewing – and liberally!

Action checklist

1 Be sure a video is really what you need.
2 Tell your producer everything they need to know about your organisation and your objectives in making the video – and be totally honest with them.
3 Let the producer ask questions, and give you suggestions and alternatives.
4 Don't give authority over the producer to anyone else but you, or a small committee.
5 Define your key audience.
6 Decide how long it will run.
7 Agree with the producer that you can pull out at either of two stages: the treatment or the shooting script.
8 Get the producer to give you a detailed budget breakdown.
9 When you see the roughcut, only comment on errors or omissions of fact or policy.
10 Do not alter anything in the commentary, except for errors or omissions of fact or policy.

Thought-starters

1 *What is the worst corporate video you have seen? Why was it so bad?*

2 *Have you ever been involved in making a video that shouldn't really have been made (went out of date too fast, never got used etc.)?*

3 *Do you enjoy watching videos at presentations? If so, why?*

4 *Do you think that the sponsor should become deeply involved in making a video beyond the areas of concept, fact and policy, and cost?*

5 *If you were making a video to include in a one and a half hour presentation, what do you think should be its maximum length? what about an all-day presentation?*

Appendix I
Summary

■ ■ ■

Summary of procedure

■ ■ ■

1   Convene first meeting

Invite:
- Expert on the subject
- Expert on the audience

2   First planning meeting

Purpose:
- To formulate precise objectives
- To formulate desired audience response
- To select a presentation team
- To draft a logical sequence
- To decide audience size and who should be invited (where applicable)
- To choose a location (where applicable)
- To fix the date (where applicable)

Action
- Book location for dress rehearsal and presentation
- Invite the audience
- Fix the next meeting
- Invite presentation team to next meeting
- Circulate to all members of next meeting the decisions (above) taken at this one

3   Second planning meeting

Purpose:
- To work through the logical sequence
- To confirm the running order, duration and breaks
- To agree each presenter's objective
- To agree each presenter's content
- To discuss major demonstrations for inclusion
- To discuss supporting documentation
- To list future meetings and their purpose, including date of run-through

Action
- Initiate preparation of major demonstrations
- Initiate the writing of supporting documents
- Initiate logistics, e.g.:
  welcoming arrangements
  meals and refreshments
  transport
  displays
  folders
  etc.
- Fix next meeting with all concerned
- Invite probable member of audience

Action each presenter
- Appoint understudy
- Write out full notes of intended content and send them in before next meeting

4   Third planning meeting

Purpose:
- To go through all the presenters' notes
- To eliminate contradiction, overlap and gaps
- To discuss all presentations from point of view of audience and see where this will necessitate omission, expansion or contraction
- To cross-fertilise, and give all presenters a chance to make suggestions about the whole presentation

Action

- Fix production session with each presenter and the production manager

Action each presenter

- Dictate presentation into tape-recorder (maximum duration two-thirds of allotted time) and get it transcribed
- Write in suggested audio/visual aids

5 *Production sessions with each presenter*

Purpose:

- To establish duration of each presentation
- To make any necessary cuts
- To ensure each presentation is well structured
- To ensure proper texturing
- To check presentations against attention curve
- To discuss content and initiate production of all audio/visual aids

163

Action

- Order all audio/visual aids and establish their delivery date
- Give final script instructions to presenter
- Fix date for stagger-through when all audio/visual aids are ready

Action each presenter

- Finalise script, and check it is within the duration allotted

6 *Stagger-through with each presenter separately*

Purpose:

- To check that all the visuals are correctly executed
- To ensure that visuals fit smoothly into the structure and script of the presentation
- To recheck timing now that visuals are included
- To enable presenter to identify any problems presented by visuals
- To judge if each individual presentation will achieve the objective for which it was devised

Action
- Final cuts, alterations, corrections to or omission of visuals

Action each presenter
- Polish up the presentation and rehearse complicated visual sequences privately with understudy

7 Run-through with everyone present including audience representative

Purpose:
- To see the entire presentation at the actual speed at which it will run
- To establish final timings
- To judge the overall effect of the presentation
- To test out all junction-point procedures
- To make final cuts or alterations that may be required
- To practise all technical and stage management details in conjunction with the presenters – lights, visuals, demonstrations etc.

Action
- Take times and make notes for each presenter
- Go through them separately with each presenter at the end. No interruptions

8 Dress rehearsal

Purpose:
- To test the whole presentation in the actual location, under the actual conditions, and with the actual equipment
- To familiarise the presenters with the circumstances they will encounter
- To give everyone practice and confidence

Action
- Times and notes as at run-through

9 *Presentation day*

- Arrive in good time
- Each presenter check through their own audio/visual aids
- Informal meeting between presenters and audience (if possible)
- Take technical upsets light-heartedly

Action

- Meet a week later and discuss the lessons that can be learned

Checklist
■ ■ ■

Structure

- Is it too long?
- Do the first two minutes set the right tone for the speaker's acceptance by the audience?
- Does the argument start from the audience's level of knowledge, interest and understanding?
- Does a clear reason why the audience should be interested emerge early enough? Does it make them want to know?
- Are there enough intermediate summaries and signposts?
- Is there too much straight, factual assertion?
- Is it too comprehensive? Are there too many details which should be in supporting documents?
- Is the last sentence the right one to leave in the audience's heads?

165

Texture

- Are there intriguing peeps behind the curtain?
- Could the audience be brought into the presentation in some way?
- Are the visuals spaced for best interest-sustaining?
- Are there long, dull patches? Can the middle trough be raised by any questions or participation?

- Does it contain too much visual dodging about?
- Are the most important points sufficiently memorable?
- Can they be given special impact? Are there pictures of everything that we want remembered?

Use of words

- Does it sound as if a written document is being read out?
- Are there any 'literary' phrases that no one ever says in conversation?
- Is it studiously avoiding 'I' and 'you'? Is it over-grammatical?
- Is the word order right for easy understanding?
- Are there enough questions stated before answers are given?
- Are the sentences too long? (Look suspiciously at anything of more than two or three lines)
- Are there too many abstract nouns?
- Are there enough examples and analogies?
- Does it assume too much knowledge? Is it insultingly oversimplified? Should more background facts be casually dropped in?
- Does it repeat itself? Is it padded out with unnecessary verbiage?
- Is it clear and unambiguous?
- Is it too cryptic and compressed?

Delivery

- Are they speaking loud enough?
- Are they avoiding eye-contact with the audience?
- Do they drop their voice at the end of sentences? Is their chin too close to their chest?
- Do they tend to gabble, mumble, or talk at the flip chart?
- Any distracting physical or verbal mannerisms? (But don't worry unless they really do distract)

Audio/visual aids

- Is the visual aid necessary?
- Is it genuinely visual or just a visible verbal?

Prepared flip charts
Drawings clear enough? Large enough? Simple enough? Interleaves included?

Flip chart
Pen colour? Presenter's positioning? Long spells of drawing? Properly stable? Sheet disposal – waste box nearby?

Whiteboard
Board properly cleared?

OHPs – operation
Noise of fan? Obstruction of vision?

167

OHPs – content
Too verbal? Too much information included? Too visually complicated? Too crowded? Sufficient use of colour? Unnecessary slides? Missing slides? Left on screen too long? Properly explained by presenter?

Slides
Spare projector? Duplicate slides? Proper rehearsal time for actual projector? Do slides fit? Rehearsal for projectionist? Agreed signals to projectionist? Agreed breakdown procedures? Avoid reloads of slides. Use of pointer.

Build-up visuals
Build-up too slow? Too many pieces to search through?

Physical objects
Are there enough? Could there be more displayed or distributed?

Working models and demonstrations
Will they be there in time to check them properly and take action if they fail? Is there time for sufficient rehearsal with them? Fire regulations, power supply, ventilation?

Tape-recordings
Check all equipment? Don't rely on automatic stops. Set sound levels in advance?

Video
Is it really appropriate? Don't run it too long. Must be correctly placed for maximum interest and effect

Audience

- Right number? Too many? Too few?
- Are presenters experienced with this size?
- Should the presentation be given more times to fewer people?
- Do you want them compact or scattered? Lights on or off?
- Proper deference by speaker?
- Wrestling or judo?
- Questions or no questions? If so, when?

One-person presentation

- Encourage questions throughout. Proceed by dialogue
- Plan the order of points to be made
- Informal rehearsal
- Prepare introduction
- Extreme simplification of visuals

Venue

- Own building if possible
- Avoid too vast a room
- Wide or narrow frontage for seats?
- Not too wide gap between speaker and front row
- Check technical facilities
- Signpost rooms and corridors
- Distractions from doors and windows – is presentation at the right end of the room?
- For strange venue, check with someone who has used it

Dress

- Are presenters dressed appropriately?
- Are they smart and well presented?
- Don't let appearance overpower the message
- Avoid extremes of fashion, tight clothes, revealing clothes, new clothes, jewellery that jangles, strong perfume or aftershave

Stage

Lights

Are all charts and speakers clearly lit? Light spill on screen? Light in speakers' eyes?

Decor

Coloured drapes or flats? Uniformity of furniture? Display panels?

169

Layout

Sightlines – check for masking. Does the stage look appetising?

Stage management

What happens at junction points? Microphone procedure. Video order and cues. Slide order and cues. Charts etc. to be set or struck during presentation? Doors closed and warning notices on outside. Go right through full script for every requirement. Ask the 'what if ...?' questions. Chalk, string, PVC tape, wire etc. Check for internal interruptions – fire drill etc. – and external – school playground outside window etc.

Appendix II
Sample presentation

■ ■ ■

For those who are interested to see how some of the principles in this book might be applied in practice, I have included the following sample presentation. I've deliberately kept it simple and made it an example of a presentation by a single presenter to a small group, but of course it could equally be a section within a larger presentation.

As you see, the left-hand side of the page indicates the principle being illustrated, and the right-hand side is a (fictitious) presentation by a manager to the board of their company on the subject of a new company pension scheme. The pension presentation has been based on the needs of a small company employing mainly young staff.

1 PREFACE **Opening courtesies**	**PRESENTER** First of all I would like to thank the board for giving me what has turned out to be a much more interesting project than I expected when I took it on
Disclaim excessive authority **Give relevant personal experience**	As you know I'm not an expert on pension schemes, although I have been administering the present scheme for the past three years
State the intention of the presentation in terms of the listeners' interest **Outline the course of the presentation with timings: 'route map'**	You asked me to review our present staff pension arrangements and make proposals. What I suggest – if you're happy? – is that I give a brief run-down on the present scheme, then look at the various kinds of scheme we might move to, and then suggest two

Give the 'rules of the road' – when you want to take questions, whether interruptions are permitted

Get them nodding

possible alternative schemes, if only as a discussion starter. That should take about fifteen minutes, and I do hope you'll stop me if there's anything you don't follow; but if it's a general point it will probably save time to keep it for the discussion session. Is that all right?

---

2 POSITION

'As you know' enables you to tell those who don't without offending those who do. If the audience knows more about the present position than you do, this is the place to ask 'feedback' questions to check if you've got it right

So, if I might start with the present scheme, as you know It dates back to when the company was fairly new andquite a lot smaller. It's a very basic, minimum scheme: the company pays in 5 per cent of each employee's salary each year into an accumulating fund which provides insurance cove while they are at work and a pension when they retire

---

3 PROBLEM

'Something around' and 'on average' enable you to omit a lot of unnecessary detail and tedious qualification

The problem is that this only provides a pension of something around 17 per cent of final salary on average, and this is beginning to prove a stumbling block when we try to recruit new staff. It's also causing an increasing amount of resentment among our existing staff, especially the more senior ones, when they find out the more generous pensions their friends in other companies are getting. But of course the principal reason for undertaking this review was the clear feeling of the board that they would like to do more for the staff, now that the company is more firmly established and profitable

Attribute to your listeners the highest motives you can manage without choking

Show when you have reached the end of a paragraph

So that's the present position: the board is not satisfied with the current level of pension it offers to its staff and wants to look at ways of improving it

Another place for an early 'feedback' check	Any questions so far – anything I've got wrong or left out?

---

4 POSSIBILITIES

Show you are starting a new section	Right. So what are the options? You can get bogged down in endless detail over this, and someone is going to have to in the end – probably me. But as far as the board is concerned, there are just three major policy decisions.
Simplify the choices – leave the secondary class for later discussions	
A visual aid on the three decisions could help in showing the listeners where they are going – and later in reminding them where they are	*1 What Type?* Final salary or money purchase? *2 How Funded?* Contributory or non-contributory? *3 How large?* What percentage of total salaries should go into the fund?

173

Let me take them in turn. First, what type? A final salary scheme aims to provide the employee with a pension   of – usually – one-sixti-eth of their salary at or near retire-ment for each year with the com-pany. So someone who has worked thirty years retires on half their final salary, thirty-sixtieths. A money purchase scheme doesn't guarantee any specific income – it builds an accumulating fund, and the employee gets a pension based on what ever size their fund has reached when they retire

Visual aid

	Premium	Pension
Final salary	Variable	Fixed
Money Purchase	Fixed	Variable

You can see the difference on this chart: the final salary scheme has a variable premium and a fixed formula for calculating the pension, while the money purchase scheme has fixed premium and a variable pension

Note how the jargon-type phrase 'open-ended' commitment is immediately translated in plain English and clarified with an example

Always put the alternative you are proposing after the one you are rejecting

The drawback with a final salary scheme – for our company at this stage of its development – is that it is an open-ended commitment: the company cannot know in advance how much it may have to pay, to keep up with inflation, say, especially in a bad year. On the other hand, as a small company, with a money purchase scheme, you know where you are; it's limited to a fixed percentage of the payroll. In practice, more and more companies of our size are going for money purchase schemes, and everyone I've spoken to recommends that type for us because so many of our staff are under thirty

Make it clear that you are moving to a new section: if you are using a visual aid, this is where you change from 1 to 2

'Chipping in' is the sort of colloquialism that helps a personal presentation but would be out of place in a written report

Second, should it be contributory or non-contributory? Again, it would be nice to guarantee everyone generous pensions without their having to make any personal contribution, but that sort of commitment is usually beyond the reach of companies our size. In fact 80 per cent of all schemes include an employee contribution, and apart from giving them a very good tax-free method of saving, a lot of companies find that it involves employees more in the scheme if they are chipping something in themselves

Starting a new section again
Simple visual aids:

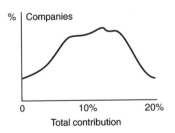

% | Companies

0   10%   20%
Total contribution

Finally, how much? This is really two questions – how much in total, and then, what proportion of that total should be the company's contribution? First, how much in total? Well, taking 5 per cent of the company's salary bill as the minimum and 20 per cent as the most generous, this chart shows the estimated distribution for companies of under fifty employees. As you

25%   100%
Proportion paid by company

Tell people they'll be getting copies, or some will draw it for themselves and miss what you're saying

see, anything over 16 per cent is fairly rare, and the broad mass of companies fall into the 8 to 16 per cent range. And second, what proportion? This other chart shows what percentage of the total those same companies contribute: again you see that most companies fall into the 65 to 75 per cent range. I'll be distributing copies of both these charts in a moment

---

5 PROPOSAL

Summarise where we have got to at the start of a new section, and where we are now going

Make it clear you are not telling your superiors what to do. Re-emphasise that you are looking at the question from *their* point of view and addressing yourself to *their* interests

Visual aids repeated with new element. Note that its complexities are easy to follow because the audience has already assimilated the basic charts

So the two decisions that really need to be taken are, first, what should be the total percentage of payroll allotted to the pension scheme, and second, how much of that should be paid by the company and how much by the employee? Of course if is for the board to balance out its desire to be generous with its need to ensure that the company will not find itself, at some future date, short of funds it needs to run the business. So what I have done is to prepare examples of two schemes at different levels, with a calculation of how each of them would have affected the company's accounts over each of the past three years, making allowance for the tax savings, obviously. On Scheme 'A' employees would receive something around X per cent of final salary average, on Scheme 'B' something around Y per cent of final salary average. As you see, proposal 'A' would put us about here on the chart of total contribution, and proposal 'B' would put us up here. And on the chart of employer's share, proposal 'A' puts us here and proposal 'B' puts us here. But, of course, these are just

175

State the next action point and target date, followed by a benefit to them if these are met

examples, and you might opt for a larger total plus a smaller employee contribution, or vice versa. You may also wish to opt for further improvement in the pensions paid to senior staff. But if we could have that board decision by the end of the month, we'd be able to work out a complete scheme for approval by Christmas, and that could be ready for introduction at the start of the next financial year

---

6 POSTSCRIPT

Circulate details on separate typescript after the end of your presentation

Obviously I've left out an enormous amount of detail – transferability, surviving spouse pensions, death in service benefits, indexation, voluntary extra contributions – but you'll find it all in the folders alongside the financial calculations. You'll also find examples of other sample companies, and copies of the diagrams I was using. And there's some literature from the three insurance companies I've been talking to – the three our brokers recommended

Closing courtesies

And that's really it. Thank you all for listening so patiently, and if you have any questions I'll do my best to answer them. Thank you.

(This pension presentation was prepared with the help of Provident Mutual.)

Index

■　■　■

the Institute
of Management

FOUNDATION

PITMAN
PUBLISHING

MANAGEMENT SOLUTIONS SERIES

The Institute of Management & Pitman Publishing
Management Solutions Series provides you with the know
how you need every day of your working life. These books rep-
resent core business skills. Not only will they help you day to
day but, if you read the whole series, you will have an impres-
sive skills portfolio to help you gallop up the career ladder.

Titles in this series

Tough talking

How to handle awkward situations.

First things first

Time management and more.

Manipulating meetings

How to get what you want out of meetings.

Thinking on your feet in negotiations

Become an expert negotiator, able to handle every situation.

How to write reports and proposals that get results

If you want your ideas to be accepted don't just write good
reports, write ones that get read and get the results you want.

The Institute of Mangement's mission is to promote the development, exercise and recognition of professional management. The Institute's members include all levels of management from students to chief executives. The Institute of Mangement supports its own Foundation, which provides a unique range of services designed to develop, inform and advise managers in every sector of business.

What has been said about **Pitman Publishing/Institute of Management** Books:

"Practical guidance on a wide range of management issues"
– *The Independent on Sunday*

"They meet the need for managers to learn fast and to solve problems quickly"
– *Professional Manager*

"These books are presented in a crisp, approachable format and offer practical guidance... The principles articulated in these books are important"
– *The Independent*

"Written in an accessible and jargon free style. Packed with helpful advice tips and tricks"
– *Business North West*

"For Busy managers with little time for training, these quick to follow guides will help develop the skills to ensure they are the best in the business"
– *Jeremy Kourdi, Institute of Mangement*

"certain to become a lifeline for managers"
– *Commerce Magazine*